Memoir of

A Small Chinese Woman

银小虎回忆录

Introduction

"Honey, Jim from upstairs just emailed me," I told my husband David with eagerness. "He made great suggestions for me, he said that I almost have a publishable book…"

"Then you can make a million dollars when your book is published," David said in his usual slow, a matter of fact manner.

"Honey," I put up my index finger over my lips, and said in a low voice, "You cannot say that! You cannot say that you write a book to make a million. That sounds bad."

"OK, you cannot say that," David backed down. "But it will be nice to make some money from the book." He still wants to remind me of a possible reason for writing this book.

Now, why did I write my stories? There are several reasons. I have told my stories of China many times to my friends outside China. Every time when I finished my stories, the response would always be: "You should write a book of your life!" or "You can make a movie from your stories." Thus fantasies planted in my mind, even Steven Spielberg's name was in my fantasy: he would be the director of my movie …. We all have fantasies!

Some people said that writing is a self-healing therapy, and that may be true. By telling people my stories, I was healing my own wounds. For years, I often had sad dreams. My ex husbands frequently haunted me in my dreams, but since I wrote my stories down on paper (on computer), they faded away from my dreams. Will I meet them in my next life, I hope not. (Only Albert, I still feel that life with him is unfinished; occasionally, we still meet in dreams, with unfinished regrets.)

If it was just for self-healing, there was no need to publish my stories. David said: "All presidents have books published, like George Bush, Bill Clinton. Movie stars had books published too." I am not a president, I am not a movie star, I am an ordinary Chinese woman. Though my stories are not heroic, nor historic, I feel they can still inspire people: *dare to dream in life, and keep trying.*

Acknowledgement

My forever gratitude goes to *Deng Mingdao*, my writing mentor, who made this book possible. Probably a decade ago, while I was living in Bahrain, Middle East, I happened to read his book *356 Dao*. I resonated with his book so much, as I felt we were on the same brain wave. Finally I sent him an email telling him how I appreciated his book. In that e-mail I mentioned that I had a desire to write, but I was not trained in writing in any way. I was surprised that as a well established writer, *Deng Mingdao* wrote back to me not only encouraged me to write, but also offering to look at stories I wrote. Later I found that we even share the same interest in Chinese martial art.

During the course of the next few years, I sent him the stories I wrote, and he always graciously replied and guided me. The most important advice, which also happened to be the first piece of advice from him was: "Do not tell people stories, show them the stories."

Without *Deng Mingdao*, there would be no completion of this book. I also want to thank many of my friends with whom I shared the draft of this book. Their feedback was always encouraging, which led to the final entry to Amazon.com.

Table of Contents

Chapter 1

Growing Up In Benxi

I grew up in a protected, easy environment. My father was a high-ranking official at China Metal Ministry in Beijing. Before Beijing, he was also a high-ranking officer in the Red Army before the Communist Party of Mao liberated China from *Jiang Jieshi*. My father joined the Communist Party when he was only a teenager. Later he was Chairman Mao and Premier *Zhou Enlai*'s personal driver.

My father came from Hubei, a southeastern province by *Yangtze* River. I never had the opportunity to visit the village where he grew up. He told me that if I went back to his village, asking about my grandfather by his name, the village people would not know him, because most of the people in the village knew my grandfather by his nickname *Clay Pot Wu*.

The village tradition was to cook pork for the family to celebrate on Chinese New Year, but my grandfather could not afford a piece of pork to provide for his family. He would climb to the hills outside the village, catch a wild dog, and killed it for meat. Thus he could provide his family for the occasion of the Chinese New Year.

According to the local tradition, dog meat cannot be cooked on the stove in the house, because it would bring back luck to the house. He dug a pit in the ground outside the house to cook dog meat in a clay pot hung over the fire.

As time went by, the villagers all called him *Clay Pot Wu*, and his real name was gradually forgotten. I can understand why my father joined the Communist Party at that young age. A Chinese saying goes: *qiong ze si bian*: Being poor can inspire a man to rebel.

My father had to change his family name *Wu* to *Fang* after he joined the Communist group, so that he would not bring any harm to his family back in the village. He kept his official name *Fang Gang* for the rest of his life, though all our children later on changed our family name back to *Wu* to honor our lineage from the small village in Hubei province in southeast China.

In 1997, my father was diagnosed with cancer. I did not have money to fly back to China to see him. When I talked to him on the phone, he offered to buy me a ticket, but I declined, I could not bear to let my father pay the bill when I was a grown up, and had been gone from China for over 20 years living in many countries. That was the last time I talked to him. Father died two months after that phone call.

The memories of my early childhood are vague, my clear memories starts from the time of elementary school when I was 7 years old. Earlier than that, the memories are only fragments. I tried past life regression a few times, but I could not even go back to childhood, much less past lives.

Though I was always interested in science, I am also interested in science beyond the conventional realm; I like paranormal, metaphysics… It makes more sense to believe that life is larger than our five senses, life has to be multi-dimensional, far beyond the five senses, time, space and matter.

My memories of life start in Beijing. We lived in the western suburbs, which is now considered the Inner city, a prime location for real estate. We lived in a 3 story apartment building, where each building has 6 units. The families who lived in those apartments all worked for different government ministries at high levels.

I was No. 2 of all the children born into my father's family. There were 4 girls, and the youngest one was a boy. He was spoiled by our grandmother *Nainai* and aunt *Baibai*. My father never had a chance to go to school, he learned reading and writing during his service in the Red Army.

My mother came from the northeastern region, which was also called Manchurian, during Japanese occupation of that region. My mother is from the Manchu ethnic group. Her father was a well-to-do farmer, so she was sent to schools and she finished high school in that region.

When the Communists defeated the *Guomindang* in the northeast region, my father left the army to take charge of a large steel complex in Benxi city of Liaoning Province. He was already in his 40's when he finally left the army that was when my mother was introduced to him. They got married and started a family. The government gave him a big house left by the Japanese before they were driven back. My father sent guards back to his native village in the south to bring his mother and sisters all to Shenyang. With a high position, he had a driver, and a gardener. Soon after my mother was married to him, we four girls were born, almost one year apart. We were all brought up by wet nurses.

Years later, when I was in my 30's, I met my wet nurse, and she recalled how difficult I was as a baby. She had to hold me all the time; she could not even put me down to eat, because I would cry.

A few years later, father was promoted to work in China Metal Ministry in Beijing, and the whole family moved to Beijing.

On weekends, my father would take us to the No.1 Department store in downtown *Wangfujing* street, and he would buy us clothes, or fabric to take home to sew dresses for us. Hand stitched! Yes, he learned sewing and knitting skills during the Long March period. The Red Army had to be self-sufficient. They could spin cotton, or wool, to make their own clothes. All of us from the older generation know a famous song *Nan Ni Wan*, depicting that era. The song is about my father's 359th Brigade's self sufficient endeavor at Yan'an, the settlement of Red Army at that time. It is a revolutionary song written in 1943 with lyrics by playwright and poet *He Jingzhi* and music by *Ma Ke*. It was made popular by the Communist Party and continues to be one of the most recognizable songs in China; some of the lyric goes: Nanniwan, everywhere is like Jiangnan (southern of Yangtze), learning again to cultivate, the 359th Brigade sets the example, let us go forward, to offer flower blossom …

My father was very good at sewing and knitting. All our girls always wore beautiful sweaters with elaborate patterns. On the other hand, my mother could not sew a button; I never saw her handling a needle.

Chapter 2

A Rebel in the Family

I remembered the time spent in boarding kindergarten, we were only at home on weekends. Both my mother and father were working, my aunt *Baibai* took care of running the household and took care of *Nainai*, my grandmother. *Nainai* and Aunt Baibai were bad in the way that they only show their affection to No.1 *Qing-nian*, my elder sister and the No.5 *Xiaorui,* the only boy in the family.

My father was always away in Chengdu, the capital of Sichuan Province in southwest part of China, Xiao-rui was the only male in the household of 7 females. Of course he was a spoiled brat by *Nainai* and *Baibai*. Cookies and cakes were all locked up in the cabinet and only *Qing-nian* and *Xiao-rui*, the two elites, could ask for goodies at anytime. For the rest of us girls, cookies and candies were a rare occasional treat.

Qingnian (*Youth* in English, because she was born on May the 4th, the International Youth Day), the No.1 girl in the family, was their favorite, because *Qingnian* was brought up by *Baibai* and *Nainai*. As for me, *Shaonian* (*Youngster* in English because I was born after *Youth*), the No. 2; and *Shaohua*, No. 3; and *Heping*, No. 4; we were all brought by nannies. We all called Qingnian: *"Jiejie"*, which means elder sister,.

Qingnian had the total power over the rest of us 3 girls; anything she said, we had to obey unconditionally. Her sovereignty ruled us till I was past 10 or 11 years old. Then one day, *Qingnian* ordered me to hand over my toy, because she wanted it, and somehow I did the unthinkable: I said:" No." She could not believe it. She was dumbfounded, as well as the other two girls. After a couple of seconds, *Qingnian* ordered me to hand over the toy, I said "No" again, this time, she ordered *Shaohua* and *Heping* to help her take the toy off my hands.

The one and only physical fight between our girls broke out. Our bodies intertwined together … one against 3, I fought hard to the end. I only remember that my new pale apple green polyester blouse (the polyester was just introduced into China, it was cool to have a polyester blouse) lost one sleeve, and a few buttons!

In our family, we were all polite to each other. My parents never raised their voices when they spoke. They never beat us, we grew up all polite, but after that unthinkable physical fight, at the cost of one sleeve and a few buttons of my fashionable polyester blouse, I gained freedom!

 I no longer had to say yes to *Qingnian* any more. She could no longer order me around. We were on even ground from that day on, and it has stayed that way till this day. A sleeve for freedom, that was a fair trade.

In the early sixties, there was a severe famine in China, and many people were starving. I do not have statistics of how many Chinese people actually died from that famine. The government probably kept it in secret. We all heard of stories of how starved people commit crimes just to fill their stomachs. Stories like this: on *Wangfujing* street, the No.1 shopping street in Beijing, a man broke the store window with a rock, to grab the cake on display, to eat. He was so hungry that he could not stop shoveling cakes into his mouth, until his stomach burst and he collapsed in front of the crowd before the police came.

Though my father was in a high position in the government office, we too felt the effect of the famine. The normally polite, quiet family was not polite, quiet at the dinner time: quarrels, accusations, finger-pointing became a daily ritual by the table: who was eating more than her quota.

The government issued food coupons for all families. Adults were given more coupons than children. I think it was less than 15 kg for an adult for staples a month. With coupons, you could buy flour or rice, or you could buy food in a restaurant. You always had to use money plus coupon to buy food on the street. Money alone could not feed your belly, coupons, coupons!

Yes, food was rationed. Each household fed their family to the ration accordingly. My father found a way to stretch out our ration: he would roast the flour, then make a thin porridge. Because rice was rationed so much, we saved rice only for occasions when we had meat on the table. The roasted flour porridge with mostly water content could quickly fill up the stomach. I still remember the aroma drifting out of the kitchen when father was roasting the flour.

My mother's creative way to cope with food shortage was to stay away from the dinner table so that her ration could be shared between children. She would return home late deliberately, telling us that she had already had dinner at work. My mother was a pharmacist working at *Jishuitan* Hospital at that time. We did not know that she did not eat at work. Instead, she would stop on the way home, buy a bottle of beer, and drink the beer to feel full. As far as I remember, food was rationed; but beer, wine, and liquor were never rationed. That was the only time my mother drank alcohol.

Often a quiet family changed into a parliament debate session at the dinner table. Imagine five children, each accusing another of eating too fast in order to get the next fill, or one of eating more than her quota.

One evening at the dinner table, Xiaorui, my brother, pointed his finger at me, accusing me eating more than my quota. Strong feeling of unjustly and wrongly accused rose up inside me: I thought to myself: The elite two (No.1 and No.5) could eat the cakes purchased with our quota, yet he was accusing me. Xiaorui continued his finger pointing, not sensing that the volcano of my feelings was smoldering underneath my tightly pressed lips.

All of the sudden, I jumped up from my chair, picked up my rice bowl, and threw the bowl of boiling hot roasted flour porridge against his face! The screaming erupted from everyone at the table; *Nainai*, *Baibai*, and all the girls. Xiao-rui tried to wipe the hot porridge from his face, but the sticky porridge was too hot to touch ... I knew that hell was broken loose by me, I dashed toward the door, I flung open the door, and started running, running fast ...

Their voices followed behind me:"Get her, get her...." I do not remember where I ran toward, but I stayed out that night, and did not return home until early next morning, when everyone was still asleep. Luckily, Xiaorui did not have scars from that episode. My family all knew that Shaonian, although was a quiet girl (*laoshiren*), don't push her to a corner.

When I was young, I was more introverted than I am now. I could stay at home for the whole day, in and out of the rooms with other members around me without speaking a word. Later in life, especially when I had my own businesses to run in order to survive in society, life changed me, Now I can talk to people, and talk to my family easily.

Chapter 3

English Study

In our family, there were no intellectuals. My father came from a humble background, but he learned read and write in the Red Army. My mother had high school education, and later she was trained as a pharmacist. The other two members of the family, Grandma Nainai and Aunt Baibai, never had any schooling.

At the end of elementary school, we would take municipal exams in order to enter to a high school. You would fill out a High School Application form to indicate what three schools were your choices.

After the entry exams, you would then be assigned to a high school, according to your exam results. On the list of high schools to choose, there were a couple of special schools. One of them was Beijing Foreign Language School. It sounded exotic to me!

At that time, China was behind the Iron Curtain, so we did not see any Westerners on the street in the city. Occasionally, if we saw anyone with a Caucasian face in the street, we would say: "Sulian ren (Russians)!" That was the only foreign influence we had.

In the early 60's my father was assigned by the government to build China's first seamless steel pipe plant. The production line

...s imported from Hungary, and the Government chose Chengdu in Sichuan province as the location for this plant. We no longer saw our father often, as he would go to Sichuan (a province in southwest of China) for months. When he came back, he came with big fruits from that region. One day he came with beautiful postcards, a doll, gifts given by engineers from Hungary. We huddled together to examine the doll, and her ethnic dress, "Hey, look at her shoes, they even have the tiny nails on the shoes." I ran my fingers over the shoes, and gazed at those beautiful postcards. With their unusual architecture, they looked like fairy land…

My father was in Beijing when I was preparing my high school entrance exams. He said that he knew the principal of Beijing Foreign Language School. He said: "You can put Beijing Foreign Language School as your first choice. I will pass a word to the principle." I was delighted.

So it was settled: my first choice-Beijing Foreign Language School, second choice-No. 6 Girls School, the last choice-No.56 High School. No. 56 high school is a local co-ed school: you could be admitted even if you flunked the exam. The fact was all my other sisters ended up in No.56 High School. I was the scholar in the family; I always liked to study. I did not need an adult to tell me to study; I always had good grades in school.

The municipal exam came and passed, and I felt pretty good about it. Then I received a letter from Beijing Foreign Language School asking me to be there for an oral exam! When I went, they asked me to choose a language. I had no idea of foreign languages. Only there and then I found out that most students for the oral exam were from the elementary school affiliated with Beijing Foreign Language School; they already learned their language of choice at their elementary school.

Since I didn't know any foreign language, they chose one for me, and told me to go for the English language exam. When my name was called, and I entered the room, there were several teachers sitting behind a row of desks. They handed me a few sheets of papers, and asked me to read them. I could not read a word, "How would I know English, this is the reason that I applied to this school," I thought.

When they realized that I did not know any English words, they asked me to follow a teacher to read those words. I failed miserably. Later I found out that my father did not speak to the principal of the School. That was my fate; in the end I entered No.6 Girls School. it was still a good school with its entry require at 96 points out of 100 of municipal examination.

Because of the humiliating experience at the oral exam at Beijing Foreign Language School, I vowed that I would study hard to learn English when there was a chance. Since China was behind the Iron Curtain, the limited foreign influence was from Eastern Europe. Most students did not want to waste their time on English class, a useless class. Russian class was more popular.

At No.6 Girls School, there were four classes that year. Two classes were assigned to study Russian, and two classes were assigned to study English. I was in No.4 class: fate was smiling on me this round; No.4 class was assigned to learn English. There were two English teachers; both were men, though we were a girls school.

No.3 class's teacher was a young man in his late 20's; a hundsom man with big eyes. The girls from No.3 often showed how proud they were of their handsome teacher. On the contrary, Zhou Laoshi, our English teacher, was in his late 40's. He had small eyes, big robust round face, looked like a hippo face. We felt inferior to the No. 3 class girls.

Zhou Laoshi started teaching us phonics, which sounded boring at the beginning. In the meantime the girls in No.3 class showed us their alphabet English. They were proud again: they could write beautiful A, B, C. We class No.4 could only utter: ai, oi, ui. We asked Zhou Laoshi to teach us the alphabet, but he insisted we should start with his phonic approach.

At the time, English classes in high schools all started with the alphabet, and the phonics were only listed on the last page of the textbook. Zhou Laoshi's teaching method was experimental. The school days went on, and at the end of the first semester, there was an exciting day for Class No.4. The Beijing TV station crew came to our class to film Zhou Laoshi's class, because we were different from all other English classes in the whole city, maybe in the whole country. We finally felt rewarded, instead of feeling inferior because our teacher had a hippo face, or we could only write in phonics. We were TV celebrities, the phonics celebrities.

In the English class, everyday, when the bell rang, Zhou Laoshi walked into our classroom with his heavy body, round and perpetually red face. We would all stand up and say, "Good morning, teacher Zhou." He would say it back to us, "Good morning students." "Then we would sit down," then one of the girls would stand up, and she would start the next routine.

"Today is Monday, the weather is fine, there are 42 students in the class today, and one is absent." This was called class report. Zhou Laoshi asked everyone in the class to do this report in English in turns.

The night before my turn to do a class report, I would spend time at home, going over the dictionary to compile a lengthy story with new words, read it loud, and memorized it.

The next day in the English class, after everyone sat down, when Zhou Laoshi had finished "Good morning, students," I would stand up. I would start with routine. "Today is Tuesday …" But the 30 second routine report never stopped there. I would go on to report stories. What happened on the way to the school, on the bus, or afterschool … Zhou Laoshi would be excited, because someone was actually talking in English with a story, not a 30 second routine. His normally red face would get even more red from excitement. Someone could converse with him in English! He would encourage me with: "Go on, go on". I always waited for my report day with eager anticipation.

In life, I consider myself an "extra mile driver", I don't mind giving more time or effort to the tasks I undertake. I am a giver in life not a taker. I don't shrink from duty or problems. My philosophy toward problems is: "face it, solve it and move on."

During our English class, if Zhou Laoshi announced, "Now I'm going to ask one of you to stand up and read this paragraph of the lesson," immediately, every girl in the classroom would duck down her head. We knew the tip: no eye contact, less chance to be asked.

When Zhou Laoshi did point with his hand to one girl, she would reluctantly stand up, head buried in the book and read the paragraph in a whisper. Zhou Laoshi would walk up next to her, raise his big hand and put it behind his small ear. "Louder, louder, please, I cannot hear it," he would say.

It was always this routine: Zhou Lashi's announcement, heads duck down, Zhou Laoshi walking up, "Louder, louder." But that was not me. Often as soon as Zhou Laoshi said, "Now I am going to ask someone to read this paragraph," I would raise up my hand high and volunteer. Zhou Laoshi would say, "Wu Shao-nian, give others a chance to try."

Eventually Zhou Laoshi would call my name, and I would stand up, with my chin held high. I would close my textbook, put my hands behind me, and start reciting the paragraph! Yes, I knew my book: I often studied the new lesson before Zhou Laoshi's teaching. English was my love, my passion.

Recently when I went back to Beijing for a visit, during which I often passed Beijing Foreign Language School. After more than 30 years, it still brings a bitter-sweet memory of that dashed dream of studying in that school. But because of it, I was instilled with determination and passion to learn English. I became an elite in Zhou Laoshi's English class.

During my third year at the school, it was the summer of 1966, the beginning of the Cultural Revolution. In any Revolution, a society turns into a chaos, and Chinese Cultural Revolution was no different. Though it was not a civil war, many people were killed, the real statistics may never be revealed by the government.

I remember we heard people committed suicide at my own neighborhood. Others were killed around us, though no one in our apartment building died at that time.

One day at the market my aunt Baibai was waiting in line, one Red Guard threatened her. Baibai was so scared, she left Beijing the next day and went back to her village to hide. No one was safe, even up to the president of the country Liu Shaoqi. Most of us little people had no idea it was a power struggle between Mao and Liu, but we all fought for the idealism the government promoted.

In the end of 1968, I went to the desert in Inner Mongolia. English study did not exist in the remote corners of subconscious mind. It was at the end of the Cultural Revolution; everyone was still caught up with trying to survive through this social upheaval. Somehow my passion for English survived. All the foreign language books were banned or burned. The book stores had only empty shelves and a lot of Mao's red books. We literally lived in an ocean of red: red flags, red banners, red armbands, red books…

My high school English Zhou Laoshi completely disappeared. I never heard any news of him ever since the beginning of the Cultural Revolution. More than 20 years later, in the year 2000, I went to visit Beijing, I wrote to the Beijing Evening News newspaper, asking them to put an ad in the classifieds looking for my high school classmates. I didn't get any leads or response. The street where the school was was gone, and the city looked so different, I was a foreigner in my own home city.

When I decided to continue my English study at the labor camp in Inner Mongolia, it was an insane suicidal decision to anyone at that time. I did not tell anyone about it. I am the type of person, that if I choose to do something, I do it, I don't need anyone else's opinions. This can be a good thing and a bad thing. A headstrong person needs God on her side.

Even my journey to Bahrain seemed crazy to my home town people in Sewanee, a small quiet college town in America. Once a Chinese martial art master told me that my name, Shaonian (youngster), decided my destiny. There is a Chinese idiom: Shaonian Zhizai Sifang, which translates to: "A youngster's ambitions are at four directions." He said that meant I would travel all over the world. Well, till this day, I have not met any Chinese with the same name. I should thank my parents for giving me this name.

How would I continue my English study in a labor camp in Inner Mongolia? I did it by translating books from English to Chinese. My English teacher Zhou Laoshi vanished, my school was closed, the country was in turmoil, and anything foreign was banned or burned. After three years in the camp, while on a two-week vacation in Beijing, I found a couple of English books. I still had my dictionary at home, so I returned to Inner Mongolia with two English books and a dictionary. Thus I started my self-education in the camp.

It was not easy; I would translate line by line, page by page whenever I had time on my own, when no one was around me. In the evenings when everyone slept, I would turn on my little transistor radio and tuned it to short wave. With an ear plug, I could listen to Voice of America and BBC. It was exciting and dangerous too; if caught, I would be in prison for a serious crime.

I was always "odd" to some people. I did not follow trends or fads, and I did not care to be with a group. I am who I am; I don't need a group to identify myself. After I started my pursuit for English study in the camp, I finally finished my first hand written translated novel: *The Prince and the Pauper.* To young people at the Labor Camp, the book was a fresh breeze. We watched enough *yangbanxi*, Mao's widow's creation of revolutionary art pieces, 8 in total at the time. We watched them over and over many times, because those were the only art shows you could see in the whole country; everywhere, everybody watched those *yangbanxi* over and over.

If there was any foreign art, it was movies from Soviet Union, Romania, or Albania. The all depicted the same theme: revolutions. My hand written translation of *The Prince and the Pauper* was circulated in our camp. I would save my meager allowance to purchase notebooks to write my translated novels. During the Cultural Revolution era, general people wore clothes in army green, blue, grey color. At the camp, we wore army uniforms. Everyone was the same; no individuality, no color, no beauty allowed. There was no individual identity or expression. Somehow my secret English study gave me that chance to have an individual identity and satisfy my yarning for artistic expression.

I would buy notebooks with different plastic covers. The notebooks' plastic covers seem to have escaped the government's censoring. They were in vivid colors and designs, such as brilliant orange and delicate apple green. I would relish the pleasure of choosing them for my next translation. Youth at the camp often asked me, "Hey, Shao-nian, have you finished another chapter?" They were hooked on my hand written novels, because the novels were different from Eastern Communist Bloc movies.

Women love fashion clothes; during that era, everyone wore the same clothes in same style; choosing a notebook with vivid color or design on a plastic cover was my desire for fashion and individuality satisfied.

One night, the bugle was blown; all of sudden, the power was cut off; that meant the emergency night drill! After all, we were in the army system and trained by army officials. The routine night drill was to pack up your bedding into a neat to bundle to carry on your back and trek in the dark for an hour or so in the desert.

That night when we returned to the camp and lined up in front of *Liangzhang*, the head of the camp, he said, "We found foreign books in Wu Shaonian's room! We all know that she's a university crazy; she only wants to study and go to a university. If this was a battlefield, if the enemy line offered her a chance to go to a university, she would surely betray our country to cross the line to join the enemy!"

To them, I was a *daxuemi* (university craze). Especially studying a foreign language was a sure sign of betrayal to the Communist government. However I continued my study, but I became more careful that not to let them find my books. Often times, I could hardly wait for work to finish, so that I could rush back to my little corner in the dormitory. I always chose a corner or a separate small room for my bed, so that I could escape to my fantasy world.

A couple of years later, when my Chinese husband Jin Zheng found out that I was studying English and translating novels. When he read my notebook translation of the story of love between a man and a woman, he could not stand it. He said, "How could you write this down?" Love or sex was not in our vocabulary at that time, and nobody dared to use them. We did not use any words describing emotions. We were revolutionaries; the only love was the love of loyal devotion to the Communist party, to Chairman Mao.

I think that is why I prefer English to describe my emotions and my thoughts; because in my younger years, I did not hear or learn those words in Chinese. Jin Zheng resented my passion for English study, as it was against social behavior of that era. One day, he grabbed my arm to take me to the police station to report me listening to the *Voice of America* and BBC. It would be a serious crime to listen to enemy stations from the West. His mother stopped him; she said, "Son, if she is in prison, our whole family will be ruined as well." Jin Zheng then asked me to promise him that I would never listen to VOA again. I said, "I have to lie to promise you, because I cannot stop my study."

Jin Zheng did not know that I and his sister, Jin Su, together with two other girls from the labor camp, had a scary encounter due to my English study. It was through Jin Su, whom I met at the Labor Camp, that I met Jin Zheng. One summer vacation in Beijing, we and two other girls from the camp went to the Summer Palace. While we were rowing a boat on *Kunming* lake, we came across a boat with two foreigners in it. Jin Su and the other girls all nudged me and whispered to me, "You studied English, show us that you can speak English too." I took their challenge. I found out that they were Arabs from the Middle East. At least, I could converse with them. I was pleased.

Pulling two boats close together, we had a photo taken with them. After saying good-bye, we continued rowing our boat. When we got closer to the shoreline, one of the fishermen there pulled in his line, and called out to us. When we got closer to him, he told us that he was a police officer, and that he had been watching us all that time, though he could not hear us from the distance. We were ordered to dock the boat, and we were taken to the police station at the park. After a couple of hours of investigation, we were finally released. Jin Su promised not to tell her brother about the incident.

When I eventually left camp after ten years, and after I got divorced from Jin Zheng; I could finally study at home without worrying about someone watching me because I was studying a foreign language. My family thought I was odd, but they also knew that when I chose to do something, I always wanted to excel at it. No one in my family tried to report me to the police.

One day while waiting in a long line at the movie ticket office, I was reading my English book, and an older man behind me asked what I was reading. I told him that I was studying English by myself. During the conversation, he was moved by my determination, and he told me that he was an official translator at a government office. He took a magazine out of his overcoat pocket; it was a real foreign magazine Newsweek! He handed it to me, and after I had a glance at it, he said that I could keep it. I was thrilled; that was the first time I physically saw and touched a foreign magazine.

It was the same thrill I had when I was a little girl, when my father brought back the Hungarian doll. When I felt her clothes and her shoes with my fingers, they evoked a strong desire in me, the desire to know of or to go to see of those exotic lands beyond the Iron Curtain.

We had been living in a vacuum of Communist system for so long. I took my first *Newsweek* magazine home that day and kept it on top of my big desk, so that I could see it every day. It was a sweet satisfying feeling when I saw it, because anything foreign was destroyed during the Cultural Revolution. I even had a photo taken with me sitting by my big desk holding that *Newsweek* magazine.

Chapter 4

My High School Days

Life in No.6 Girls School was always fun and full of activities. In the mornings I was often the first one waiting outside the gate until Zhang Daoye (Big Grandpa Zhang) the watchman opened the gate. The watchman was not really old, but his shining bald head commanded some form of authority or seniority, so to call him Daye seemed proper despite that he was only in his 50's at the most.

I liked going to No.6 Girls School: it gave me the excuse to stay at the school longer, to have the freedom, to feel independent. We lived in the west suburbs (Beijing developed so much since then, it is now considered downtown).

It would take two bus routes to get to the school. Usually, I got up very early to catch an early bus. Otherwise you had to fight your way to the school. Buses would be so full, there was always a huge crowd at each bus station, everyone tried to get on, the pushing, shoving … it was awful. So I preferred to being an early bird; I didn't mind to be at the school early.

One morning, I got up, and the clock in my room read 2. I said to myself: "Well, the clock stopped." I quietly walked to my mother's room and pushed open the door. The clock on the wall in her room was ticking: 'tick, tock, tick, tock," faithfully, but it read 2 too! I thought, "Wow, both clocks stopped." I walked quietly back to my room, dressed and left the home quietly not to disturb any one as usual.

The short walk through the neighborhood buildings was always silent; I seldom saw anyone out then, only me and my shadow under the dim street light. I reached the main road and stood at the bus stop. The street was empty, which was normal, since I usually get on the first bus around 5:30. But this time, the bus did not come.

There was not a soul in the street. After a long while, suddenly I realized, "Oh, the clocks did not stop at the same time, it is me that got up at two o'clock. A bit too early!" Upon this realization, I chuckled silently and walked back through the neighborhood buildings. Under the dim street light, my shadow and my quiet footsteps were the witness of my love for school days…

I loved to be at the school the first. Once Zhang Daye opened the small side gate, I would say, "Zhang Daye, Ninzao," and squeeze pass him before the gate was fully opened.

Once inside the school, I would pass the empty playground and head to my class room in an old bungalow in a courtyard. That was before the school built a new multi story classroom building.

Our old classroom had no central heating: in winter we heated our room with a small cast iron stove.

I loved to take a couple of sweet potatoes with me to the school. I enjoyed the pleasure of lighting up the stove and putting my sweet potatoes under the bottom section of the stove. The heat and hot ashes would slowly cook the sweet potatoes. By noon time, I would have hot sweet potatoes to share with my friends. I enjoyed the silent classroom. Though in winter it was still dark outside, I preferred not to turn on the light. I loved to watch the flame glowing, to feel the warmth from the stove on my face, the smell of the sweet potato...

Because of the limited space downtown, our school did not have a regular track field for us to run. We used the small lane outside the school gate, which connected to the main streets on both ends, so you could run a circle of about 800 meters. No.4 Boy's High School was at the other end of the lane. No.4 Boys school was even more elite than us No.6 Girls School. Their average entry marks had to be 99!

We girls always wondered what the Boys' school looked like behind those high brick walls. In the mornings, I liked to run laps around the lane, because I could see those boys hurrying to their school gate. I was curious about those smart boys even though I didn't know any of them. But the world behind those high brick walls remained a mstery.

I grew up in a woman's world, as my father was always far away in Sichuan. There were 7 women in our household: my mother, my grandma, my aunt Baibai, and three sisters. The only male was my younger brother, he was a true spoiled brat. Any experience with men would have to wait untill 1968 when I went to Inner Mongolia.

In my first year at the high school, I continued my swim training with the West City District Swim Team. The swimming pool was quite far, it was at the other end of the city; I had to travel by bus, changing a few routes.

After school, I hurried to catch the bus to the east side of the city. When I got to the stadium, while waiting for our team's turn to use the pool, I would get down on the floor to do my homework. Like many sports teams, besides your good training results, we needed to keep good grades to remain on the team.

In my second year of the school, the school offered a special parachute training program during the summer break. I applied and got accepted, so I started parachute training. By the end of that summer, out of 20 girls in training, two were selected for further training for the competition. I was one of the lucky two.

The training ground was even further out to the eastern side of the city. It was too much to juggle between two sports, I had to make a choice: swimming or parachuting. I chose parachuting.

That was the end of my swimming training. Though I participated in a few competitions, I just could not envision me as a future swim star, I was too small to be a swimming star; I was always the smallest in the team, but I had good training results. The first competition I took part in was when I was still at the elementary school. I won and broke our school's record in backstroke. I was awarded a little pink book to certify that I passed the national standard set for youngster's group. I kept that little pink book for a long time; I probably lost it when I left China.

For backstroke, I always had the best time in our team. In the municipal level competition, I would swim in the relay for older age group. I liked swimming, but I never liked the competitions. Generally, I am athletic, I like to move the body, but I don't like the competitions. My parachuting training was eventually aimed for competition too: you needed to land on the target. I was proud to be a member of the National Defense Sports Club, to have a special passport of the club at a young age. That was all ended when the Cultural Revolution started in the summer 1966, the third year of my junior high school.

Chapter 5

The Cultural Revolution

The Cultural Revolution started in summer 1966, the year we were supposed to graduate the Junior High. But we never did the final exams. The Cultural Revolution disrupted normal life throughout China. It lasted 10 years. Until this day, I still don't fully understand how the power struggle in the upper level between Mao and other high ranking officials resulted in the grass root scale revolution. The effect or result was devastating. Hundreds of thousands of people were killed, persecuted, or banished from their homes to remote regions or villages. Factories stopped production, villages stopped farming, schools stopped teaching. In one sentence: the whole economy stopped. There are movies and books on that particular era called "Wound & Scar Literature", the name itself shows the vast scale of suffering for people in China.

When I mentioned to my sister that one day maybe I would write a book about my life in China during that era, she replied that with new generations, no one cares about reading Wound & Scar literature.

In my class in high school, there was a girl named *Shiqing Huang*. She was quiet most of the time, but when she spoke, she always made you laugh; she had a way of humor. *Shiqing Huang* lived in a courtyard (siheyuan) which used to belong to her family. After the Liberation, the government of the New China confiscated most of the rooms. The family only had two rooms left for themselves.

The courtyard was located in the western downtown area. It was situated halfway between my home and the school. If I wanted to walk to the school by a bee-line route: I needed to take a bus for 4 stops, then walk through a maze of small lanes to get to the school. *Shiqing Huang*'s home was just at the middle point of that route. It took about an hour to walk to the school. Sometimes, I would stay overnight with *Shiqing Huang* at her home, so that the next day I could walk to school with her.

If I went to school by bus, it took just as much time, plus I had to fight the crowd to get on the bus. Thus I spent many nights at *Shiqing Huang*'s home. When the Cultural Revolution started, everything changed. Suddenly there were class differences: 5 Red classes; which included workers, farmers, army soldiers, and revolutionary government officials; and 5 Black classes; which included capitalists, landlords, rich farmers, and rightists. The Cultural Revolution's goal was to purge the black classes from the cities.

In our class of forty-some girls, there were only 4 girls from red classes, and the rest were from Black classes. It seemed that the children in the black classes had better academic background; they entered the schools of high academic standards.

My memory of the beginning of the Cultural Revolution is vague now. I remember many parades to *Tiananmen* Square, and Mao greeting the Red Guards on that podium. We, the four Red class girls in the class, were naturally members of the Red Guards of our school.

One day before the school was finally closed and we still had our classes; during one class, a group of adults just walked into the classroom demanding to talk to our teacher. After the brief talk, the teacher announced that those people were to take *Shiqing Huang* away, because her father was a landlord, a black class family. The whole family was to be banished from the city. They were taking the family to a remote village.

Shiqing Huang, with tears in her eyes, begged that they let her stay in Beijing; she did not want to go to a village. Those people did not waste their time; they walked to her desk; they dragged her arms. She was desperate; she clasped the desk with her hands; she was crying: "Please don't take me away, don't take me away...."

After they dragged her out of the classroom, the whole class was quiet, *Huang*'s pleading voice still lingered in the classroom , and in our mind. Other girls wondered what would happen to them next because many of them were from black class families.

The Cultural Revolution spread like a wildfire. It started in high schools, soon after Mao's initiation with Red Guards on Tiananmen Square on August 18, 1966. Then it spread from schools to every corner of the country. Red Guards left schools to spread the seeds of revolutionary fire to other cities and other parts of the country. Every day, Red Guards marched on the streets searching for people of black classes and dragging them out of their homes. They shaved their heads into "Ying-yang head": only half of the head was shaved. They paraded them in the streets with a poster board hanging from their neck or hung a heavy brick with a thin metal wire...

The revolutionary fire was growing out of control. Red Guards or people who called themselves Red Guards broke into homes of black classes, ransacking, confiscating, torturing... The torturing was a daily street scene. I was not scared because I was a Red Guard. I came from a very RED family, but my heart was hurting to hear or see the beating and torturing of people. I decided to leave the Red Guard of my school. I could not join them to seek out the black class people. I did not want to lay my hands on anyone.

I did not go back to school, by then all the classes were closed anyway. Many teachers were in trouble; their heads were shaved into Yingyang heads by Red Guards; including the young handsome English teacher for class No. 3. I stayed at home; I talked to the boys and girls in our apartment building about forming our own Red Guard team since all of the families (6 in all) were government high ranking officials, all from Red class.

Thus our own team was born. We also included a few of our classmates, all from Red Class families. We decided to answer Mao's call of spreading the seeds of Revolution to the countryside.

We took the train heading south. Mao's 818 Meeting at Tiananmen Square gave the Red Guards supreme power. If you were a Red Guard, normally with red arm band printed with RED Guard on it, you could travel by train free. You could stay at other schools free, you could even eat at many places free.

It started as only Red Guards could travel around the country free, but soon people from any work units of the country were travelling free. At each train station, a train was so full, because it was free, that you could not get in through the door. As soon as the train pulled into a station, people started climbing on to the train through the windows. You could hardly get water or food on the train because of the crowded conditions.

To go to the toilet, you had to wade and step through oceans of bodies. The best seats on the train were on the top: the luggage rack, because up there, no one could step on you. When I was young, I often had a stomach ache problem. Now when we started traveling on the train, my stomach problem seemed exacerbated. I remember that during one leg of the train journey, my stomach ache was so severe, that they had to telephone or sending telegram to the next station for a doctor to be ready because I fainted on the train.

We traveled far; we would stop at one place for a few days, then continue travelling. When we stopped at Xian, it was not too far from *Yan'an*. *Yan'an* was called the cradle of the Revolution, because it was where the Red Army, led by Mao, after the infamous Long March, arrived. Mao used it as a headquarters and base. The Red Army learned to be self-sufficient: they cultivated crops, raised sheep, making wool, even waving.

My father learned all these skills; he was an excellent knitter. Years later, when he had his own family, with five children plus aunts, he always produced sweaters with beautiful patterns! My sisters and I wore those beautiful sweaters in school. We were proud, and even felt more proud when we told people that our father knitted them!

My mother, however, could not handle a needle, not to mention knitting. I must inherit my father's talent: I could sew with any patterns, I could knit any patterns. When I wore my own sweater, it always got remarks.

Eventually the Red Army defeated Jiang Jieshi's army and liberated the whole country. Jiang Jieshi escaped to Taiwan. My father followed Mao through the Long March. He was Mao's driver and bodyguard for a long while at Yan'an.

He asked to be transferred to the front line to fight like a man. Eventually, he was assigned to Division 359, which later became a legend. There was a popular song made for Division 359. The older generations all remember that song.

My father was finally serving in a real army, as a lieutenant for Division 359's logistic unit. Years later, whenever he reunited with his old army friends, they would have wine and talk about those old days in Yan'an. But he always closed the door when they talked. He never told us children about any of his life in the Red Army, or any of Mao's stories when he was his bodyguard and driver, though he knew Mao so much as Mao's driver and bodyguard. One thing I regret was that I did not have a chance to sit down with him and persuade him to tell us his stories about those years in the Red Army in Xi'an and Yan'an.

Now he is gone, his ashes are laid side by side with other old carders on the Red Army Memorial Wall in Beijing along with those never-told stories of Mao and Mao's wives.

We left Xi'an to travel by truck to *Yan'an* to visit Mao and the Red Army's historical places. The journey took several hours. It was in early winter; sitting in an open truck, we all huddled together under a blanket. It was so cold, my feet started feeling numb. Some local people in the truck told me to wiggle my toes to keep the feet from frostbite. I did just as they said, and it worked. My feet finally came back to life and eventually became warm. That was a valuable lesson I learned from that journey. It helped me many times years after.

At one village in Yanan, I was amazed to find out that some local villagers even remembered my father! That was probably 20 years after Mao's army left Yan'an.

From Xi'an, we started heading down southwest; we stopped at Chongqing in Sichuan province. Chongqing is a big city perched on the banks of the Yangtze river. At night, all the lights from buildings lit up, flickering up the mountain range. Joining the stars in the sky, the lights reflected on to the river below, which made you wonder if you were in a heaven of stars.

I would watch local farmers in awe, carrying heavy load of goods on a flat split bamboo poles, though both ends tipped down by the weight of the load. But with the farmer's dance like walking, the ends of the pole would bounce back up and tip down: up, down, up, down.

The street scene was so different from Beijing; even the air of the southwest was so different from Beijing's dry air. It felt warm and sultry, it made you feel sleepy. We stayed at Chongqing for a few days at a local college campus.

There was a room across the corridor from our room; the door of that room was always open. I could see that there was a young man lying in bed alone in that room; he seemed very sick. Later I found out that he was from a black class family, so no one cared to ask him if he needed help. I brought some food to him from the cafeteria; this act was ridiculed by my team members for "showing sympathy to a class enemy." I did not care about my team members remarks.

I had left my high school's Red Guard for the exact same reason: I could not stand cruelty to another fellow man, whether he was an enemy or friend, they are human beings like me. There was one young man in our team; he was a classmate of my upstairs neighbor. His father was a lieutenant in the army. He was cruel; on the train, he would torture old people from black classes, whipping them with his leather belt. The brass buckle hit shaved heads, and he would lough at the blood dripping down their faces. I had strong disgust toward this young man.

From Chongqing, we continued heading southwest to Zunyi in Guizhou Province. Zunyi is another historical town in Chinese

Revolution history. I remember climbing far up to a remote mining community to help "spread the fire of the Cultural Revolution".

There the climate was subtropical, with thick vegetation anywhere you looked. We were not used to the climate in that kind of environment. We were city kids. Everybody got sick from the water and food there. I had an insect bite on the top on my right foot; it got infected so bad, pus oozed out of it. I had chills all over me. We did not have any money left. Coming down the mountain, we stayed at Zunyi; we all sent telegrams to our parents back in Beijing. We were asking them to send money; we were all home sick. Waiting in the room watching the never ending tropical rain dripping down the bamboo awning, we lost our fighting spirit; we wanted to go home, back to Beijing. When the money finally arrived, we got on the train heading up north to Beijing.

When I was back in Beijing, I realized that many things had happened. A lady I knew, who lived next to our apartment building; committed suicide because she was accused as a black class by a group of Red Guards while one day walking on the street. Auntie Zhang was so scared that she hung herself in her apartment. Several days later the stench of her body alerted people.

One day my aunt Baibai was shopping at the little market just across the street from our apartment. Because of a dispute of the place on the waiting line, some young people said she was from a black class. My aunt Baibai was scared. When she came back from the market, she purchased the train ticket and went back to her village in Hubei province the following day.

When I went back to my school, most teachers were gone. They were either hiding or were sent away to villages by the Red Guards. I had not seen teacher Zhou, my English teacher, or any other of my favorite teachers ever since I left Beijing with my own Red Guard team.

I heard years later that Mr. Zhou lost his eye sight due to glaucoma. When a society is caught up in a Revolution, it's like being caught up in a tornado: life spins fast out of control. If anyone figures out the statistics of Chinese history, I wonder what the numbers would show about the suicides during the Cultural Revolution. I wonder if the number of suicides during this time could be the highest in China's five thousand years of civilization. Well, someone could get a PhD for this research. I think that it was not the physical suffering that caused such a wide spread rate of suicides, it was the sudden social status change; the public humiliation; the dignity as a human being, when threatened, or taken away; that was more unbearable than the physical challenge.

With no teachers to teach in classes, the government asked all schools to start some kind of education program. Our school sent us to a nearby village in the suburb. We all slept on the floor in one big warehouse room. The farmers put straw on the floor, and we then roll down our little beddings . It was in the middle of summer, so we did not need much for sleeping. Every morning we got up very early to help the villagers with the harvest in the field. It was early, and the sun did not rise yet. I still remember the coolness of the dew in the field; our shoes and the bottom of the pants always got wet, but later on in the middle of the day the heat from the Sun was intense.

There was a girl named Liu Lan in my class. She was from a Muslim family, the only Muslim in our class. Even her looks was different: her fair hair color, her big round eyes. She had been the assistant for Mr. Zhou in our English class. Of course, her English was good; maybe there was a silent rivalry between *Liu Lan* and me. We were never very close.

Being from a black class, *Liu Lan*'s father was beaten to death by Red Guards while I was travelling in the Southwest. She could not openly express her sadness, fearing that she would be accused of holding sympathy towards black classes. That would get her more troubles. She silently tied her hair braid with a rubber band that had white thread wrapped on it.

In China, it is a custom to pay respect to the dead with the color of white. This caused the Red Guards of my class to order her to take down the rubber band with white thread. It was sad to see people using power over lesser class people. Though I was a Red Guard, I just could not see this type of cruelty. I was born to fight for the underdogs; I could not be a top dog abusing the power. Seeing Liu Lan was forced to pull down the hair band because of white thread wound on it was too much. The next morning, when all students got up early as usual, I remained in the big hall with some vague excuse. When others left, I packed up my little bedding roll, and quietly walked off. I left the village; I left my classmates; I did not want to see any more of that, I did not want to be any part of that …

Chapter 6

Going to Inner Mongolia

By the end of 1968, almost three years after Mao initiated the Cultural Revolution, the government called all the Red Guards and all the students to return to their schools. The goal for the government was to bring the turmoil of the revolution down and normalize the school education. But there was a problem. Tens of thousands of young high school students, the would be graduates of junior and senior high schools all over the country, had been caught up in the Cultural Revolution. These students had not had the time and opportunity to study, and graduate. But now to bring normality back to education, they had to move on, out of the high school, or out of the education system. They could not go to universities, because they missed the education to qualify. Thus the government, or Mao, started another political movement; called "Shang Shan Xia Xiang." "Shang Shan Xia Xiang" translates to 'go up to the mountains and go down to the villages," which means to get your second education from real life in the countryside. The real purpose of this movement was to get the would-be graduates of the three years out of the cities, so that the new generations of students can start normal education.

The movement was very strict: 90% of all the would-be graduates in all the cities had to leave the city. There were few choices to choose: go to a village far away designated by the government; or to the Great Northeast plain to work on a big scale state run farm co-op. Some went to Tibet. If you refused to leave the city, the government would cancel your residence registration; which meant that you would have no food coupons issued to you. Without food coupons, you could not purchase any food. And our course, you could not live without food. The government did allow a very small percentage of students to remain in cities under special conditions: 1) you had a disease that made you not physically fit to live in the countryside, 2) you were recruited by government factory in that city.

When the "Shang Shan Xia Xiang" movement was issued by Mao, a lot of parents were worried. They did not want to see their kids suddenly leaving home, sent to a remote village or a state farm, but they could not save their kids either. All the schools had hard time persuading students to leave the city. One day they announced that the government textile factory was at our school to recruit for the factory. Each class could only have two students chosen. When my name was called out among the chosen ones, I could feel the eyes of envy from my classmates, wishing it was their names. The recruit team told me that they chose me because I had a very "red background:" my father was Mao's driver during the Long March period...

Though I was among the lucky ones at the school, I did not feel that way. I had been excited secretly when I heard about Mao's "Shang Shan Xia Xiang" movement. I imagined the free life in wild places, maybe Tibet...so I announced to my class and the school that I was giving up that chosen lucky position to somebody else. I wanted to leave the city, to go to the mountains or villages...the teachers were overjoyed to see a student volunteering to leave, so I was invited to step on the podium at the playground of our school. Leaning to the microphone, I waved Mao's little Red Book high, quoted his words from the Book: "You should go to exercise in strong winds and big waves." I talked of my dream of life in a countryside of big sky. The speech moved and motivated many students to sign up to leave Beijing. Afterward, some of my classmates called me a fool to give away an envied opportunity to remain in Beijing. When I went home and told my parents what I did at the school, they were not happy at all. Like all the parents, they did not want to see their children end up in an unknown village....

One night a week later, when my father came home from work, he told me something he had heard through the insider's news. The government was organizing a new setup out in the Inner Mongolia region; it would be called Inner Mongolia Production and Construction Corp. It would be managed by army officers: the whole setup would be the same as in the army; but instead of soldiers, there would be all the young would-be graduates from cities across the country. Since it was just the beginning, the hatching of the project, my father said that we could not tell others at the school. He said that through his position and connections at the government, he could get my sister Shaohua and I into this program. Shaohua is one year younger than I, so she was also a would-be graduate and had to leave the city as well. Our father told us that he'd rather see us go to this "Nei Mong Bing Tuan" (short for the Production and Construction Corp) than to an unknown remote village. At least it would be managed by real army officers. Otherwise, who knew what would happen to us young girls in a remote village.

Inner Mongolia. It sounded just like my dream of big sky country, with nomad minorities galloping on horseback in the vast grassland.... I jumped up with excitement and told my father, "Yes, please arrange it! Let me go to Nei Mong (Inner Mongolia)." I could not keep my excitement to myself; the next day, I told my classmate Yuanyuan. Since we both came from high ranking official families, and we both were trained in swimming, we were always close. Yuanyuan had the same problem as most of us. Her parents did not want to see her end up in a remote village, so she asked me if my father could add one more girl to his arrangement. I begged my father and he finally consented. A few days later, Yuanyuan told me that her elder sister Dongdong wanted to join our secret, pioneer group.... I begged my father again, and he consented. A few days later, Yuanyuan told me that Dongdong's best classmates hated to go to a remote village, could it be possible, that my father.... So I asked him again; I said, "BaBa, do a good deed, we are all good girls, please help." My father said that was the final, no more friends. So there were me, Shaohua, Yuanyuan, Donggong, two of Dong Dong's classmates; all six of us, Beijing girls, arranged to go to Nei Mong before the big setup of the Corp.

Thus, Yuanyuan and I left our school early because we told the authority of the school that we did not need school to arrange us to a village.

Our departure was in November of 1968. Since then, I have not heard, or known what happened to all my other classmates in my class. Where did they go? What happened to them? In June 2000, I was in Beijing and I wrote to Beijing Evening News newspaper. I wanted to place an ad to look for my high school classmates. But I did not get a reply from them; plus, I had a busy schedule, so I could not pursue this project. The next time I go to Beijing, I will continue to look for my school mates. In China, it is not a custom to have high school reunion. Now when you are in your 50's, it is natural that you start looking back. I hope that I can organize a class reunion one day in Beijing.

I do not have a clear memory of leaving Beijing railway station that day in Nov. 1968. I know we each had a very simple package: a bedding roll and hand bag with some washing essentials. Because it would be like in an army, everything, including uniform would be provided. The memory of arriving in *Neimong* was etched in my memory forever. The train ride was over 10 hours. We arrived there at daybreak. When I Stepped out of the train, I almost rolled down the high embankment of the rail track, because there was no platform at that small station. The town was called "Urad Front Banner", a foreign name to me. It was in the Mongolian language; there were many places there using Front Banner, Back Banner as their towns names. I was thinking "banner" was probably town in Mongolian. There were two open army trucks waiting by the railway track. An army officer in the usual army uniform, with a red star on his cap and red badges on his collar, walked up to us. He told us he was in charge of our company; we could call him Sergeant Yang.

Our luggage was thrown onto the back of the trucks. Sergeant Yang and the driver helped us climb into the back. We went through a couple of dirt streets before coming out into open land. There was a huge piece of canvas on top of us to protect us from the cold winds of a vast open land: Inner Mongolia.

From under the canvas I could see glimpses of a faraway horizon and the barren land.... It seemed to be getting colder as time went on. We all huddled together under the canvas as the truck kept going and going forever. When we finally arrived at the post, it was already dark; we could not see anything, as there was no electricity out in the desert. Quickly we rolled out of the truck and were ushered into a small room. The room was small, probably 4m X 6m. There was a raised mud platform at the other end of the room with a small mud stove connected to it. I knew it was a *kang*, a form of bed made with mud bricks. It had a duct under the platform with a mud stove built next to it, so it could be heated in cold weather. The heated air and smoke from the stove would flow along the duct beneath to heat the platform. *Kang* is a popular heating method used in villages in northern China.

Contrasted with the long hours of our truck ride journey in frigid cold and wind, the warm air in the room made us relaxed and drowsy. We rolled out our bedding on Kang, lying down next to each other. It was so quiet, and the light from the mud stove was casting patterns that were dancing on the ceiling. The only sound was coming from the fire burning in the stove. We were too tired to talk, and soon all our Beijing girls fell into sound sleep.

We woke up early the next morning, eager to see what was out there. We all got up and dressed in heavy padded coats. When I stepped out of the room, the cold morning air hit my face. I could see the morning sun, the faraway horizon.... It was so different from Beijing with its people, streets, buses. I looked up at the beautiful blue sky and flew open my arms, to embrace all this new life into me. A girl burst out, "Oh, the F-R-E-S-H air!" Right after that we heard giggling sounds coming from behind us. When we looked back, there was another room next to ours! The giggle sound soon became a loud laughter...there were BOYS behind that door! No matter who was there, we decided that we would show those boys that girls from Beijing were serious and tough. We started marching in a line; one, two, one, two, turn-around! One two, one two.... Oh, it felt like we were in a real army. This only made the laughter become hysterical. Finally, that door was opened, and out came the boys; somehow, we could see that they were not city boys. They told us that they were from Nei Mong (Inner Mongolia); the locals! They arrived a week before us. We were all the very first people before the final nationwide recruits arrived.

Our life at that first post was simple before the recruits arrived. Every morning, Sargent Yang would train us in marching formation. Then in the afternoon, we prepared more mud rooms, to be ready for the newcomers. Inner Mongolia was a dry barren land; there was no river, nor a well near us. Our water source was several miles away; an oxen wagon with a water tank would fetch water from there. Often you could see small insects swimming in the water from the tank. We ate mostly potatoes, corn, carrots and cabbage; which were very different from what people in Beijing ate. In Beijing, we ate rice, noodles, pancakes. (Corn meal was considered food for poor village people by city folk). Once a month we could have pork in a dish. All supplies were brought to our post by those army trucks. I heard that a few miles away, though we could not see it, there was another post. The Government's big plan was to fill each post with 200 young would-be graduates from cities all over the country. With Inner Mongolia's hundreds of thousands of square miles of barren land, sparsely populated; the government could easily disperse hundreds of thousands of would-be graduates.

We were waiting for the newcomers. After some days, the initial excitement of big sky, open land subsided. Life seemed changed, and we were bored. Besides a few mud houses at the post, the only excitement there was that leaky oxen wagon. The post was quiet. When we were inside the room, sometimes the fire's burning from new coal made sound pu-pu-pu-pu. It sounded like a truck's engine coming from afar. Someone would say, "Oh, I hear a truck coming!" We would all jump to our feet, fighting to squeeze out of the door to see who could first spot the truck. But the empty horizon only brought us down to the reality that the sound was from the stove. At that time, none of us envisioned that our life in Inner Mongolia would span over ten years. The night in Nov.1968, when I stepped onto that train taking me to Inner Mongolia, I did not realize that it was the beginning of me leaving childhood. From a naïve school girl in Beijing, I stepped and stumbled along into womanhood through 10 years of saga on the vast Gobi desert.

Chapter 7

Digging Irrigation Trench

In winter 1968, I arrived at an outpost for young would-be graduates from cities. I was among the first dozen young people at the post, soon, more young people arrived by truck load. Our unit was called No. 3 company, there were about ten companies to make up No. 13 Brigade, 13 brigades made our No. 2 regiments. So the number of young people scattered around whole Inner Mongolia was staggering. Of about 200 people in our company, 50% were from Inner Mongolia, and 40 % from Beijing, a few from other cities. Winter in Inner Mongolia was cold, when the wind blew, there was no land barrier, or any trees to slow down the wind. The truck ride from the railway station to our post was cold, it was common when young people from Beijing arrived at the post, some of them were already frostbite. Eventually, we were issued uniforms, with padded jackets for the cold temperature there. Since it was so cold in winter, we did not go outside much. Our regiment had agricultural assignment: we were ordered to cultivate the desert, and change it into a crop production bas0e. But winter was rigid cold, the land was frozen a few feet deep. We had to wait for the spring, for the land to thaw before we could shovel or dig.

We did not all stay inside the rooms all the time, a few times a week, we would walk in double file to another company's post. It was not an easy walk, several miles, with cold wind. We covered our heads with padded army caps and white cotton masks, so that the face would not be frostbite. Only eyes were exposed. When the warm breath hit the eye lash, the breath would freeze right on the eye lashes, we had to wipe constantly to prevent the upper eye lash from frozen together with lower eyelash. When we came back from the other post, we all looked like aged into 90 years old, our exposed hair, eye brows, eye lashes all turned white, because of frost and ice.

Finally, the spring 1969 came. The land thawed, which made driving to the railway town dangerous,: because the hard frozen road became soggy, spongy, truck could get stuck easily. So there would be days, when the supply truck did not appear, our food run out. We had to eat the only food we had: potatoes from the root cellar at the post, the potatoes already turned green because of the warm spring. Many of us vomited after eating green potatoes. Luckily, 3 days later the supply truck came. We were so happy to see cabbages, and that evening, we had pork in our dish!

With spring arriving, we started working in the field. Each morning, we got up early; no longer did we do the marching drill, or walking drill. We carried shovels, picks, walking in a single file, We had to walk several miles to the field to dig irrigation trenches and planting millet seeds in the fields.

There was no lunch out in the field, we had breakfast, then dinner when we came back from the field at the end the day. Finally, we completed the network of the irrigation trenches, now we could let water into the trench. The main trench was about 3 or 4 feet wide and at least 2 feet deep. One day at the end of the day, we all walked in single file along the embankment of the main trench heading back to the post still several miles away. Long day's digging in the field, with empty stomach, we were beat. In single file, we walked, heads down, it was quiet, everyone was too tired to talk. The embankment seemed endless: the sight of water, the ugly muddy brown water, was a far cry from chlorine scented aquamarine water of the training pool I was so used to back in Beijing for my swimming trainings. It seemed so long ago and far away in history. Suddenly I was seized by a strange strong desire: "Oh, if my body could feel the water flowing again…" I deliberately lost my footing, there I tumbled down the embankment, I went straight into the muddy water. I heard screaming around me: "Help, someone fell into water!" Everyone stopped, standing along the embankment, "Don't be panic, I can swim." I called out, I started swimming along the trench, free style, backstroke… Then someone else "fell" into water, then another one, another one… soon the trench became a children's playing pool, water splashed everywhere, laughter filled the open air, drifting and faded over the silent barren land.

In the fall of 1969, despite of our large-scale water irrigation network, despite of a ton of millet seeds we planted, we did not have any crop at all. The water we poured in the field, only brought white powdery stuff to the surface. Tons of seeds were wasted. The land was simply too arid to grow any crop. The Headquarter in *Huhehaote* sent down new command. Our whole brigade, 13 companies, was ordered to change into an industrial regiment, and relocate to the outskirts of Baotou, a city of the region known for its steel and coal industries. Baotou was about 2 hours train ride toward east. It meant we would be 2 hours closer to home, Beijing. We were excited for the new assignment. We were ordered to move before winter came down again. A few trucks came, loaded with our bedding rolls, and squeezed enough young people in each load, I was happy to say Goodbye to the post there. There was no green color in the memory of my brief life at the post there. Everything seemed in monotone of brown, brown mud house, brown ox wagon, brown water, brown land...

Chapter 8

A Fire Keeper

The new location is about 200 kilometer away on eastside of Urad Front Banner, it was at the outskirt of Baotou, an industrial city in the region. Our whole brigade was changed into an industrial regiment: one company was to be set up as a rock quarry plant, one company was to set up as a fertilizer plant. My company was ordered to build a paper mill at new location; it was called *Wanshui Quan* which meant A Thousand Springs! The location is supposed to have a vast water aquifer.

At the new location of paper mill, I was first assigned to the squad at the cafeteria. I was ordered to be a fire keeper. At the beginning of the construction of the paper mill, the cafeteria was temperately set up in a building used as the warehouse of raw material. The kitchen was at one end of the warehouse. There were two big stoves made from mud bricks. They were about one meter high platform up upon the ground with gigantic cast iron woks; each was of 1.5 meter diameter sitting in the middle of the platform. Behind the platform there was a pit; that was where I was assigned to work. My job was to keep the fire going to cook the food for the company. Being a city girl, living in a government apartment building, I never had any knowledge or experience about keeping a huge stove going. With 13 companies in our brigade, I was the only girl assigned to be a fire keeper. It was a man's job. I was told to shovel coal through an opening into a small place beneath the humongous woks. The first week was not easy for me. When the bugle was blown, about two hundred young people all filed into the middle section of the warehouse. They stood in lines with each squad. But the food was not ready, because the fire was not strong enough to cook the steamed buns. The head of the company ordered the waiting crowd to sing songs while the cafeteria squad was trying to get food ready. When they finally opened the lid of the bamboo steamers, the buns had not risen as they should have! Instead, they were a heap of sticky lumps. The hungry crowd was still singing in the front. The leader ordered kitchen staff to serve the sticky buns anyway. I dared not to walk to the front; I could hear the cursing and grumping from the crowd. Hiding behind the stove platform, down in the pit, I silently wiped the tears off my face; but my coal dust covered hands only made my face look more ridiculous. When I was working as a fire keeper, to most people on the camp, the image of me was always "a girl covered with coal dust". If one day I was not covered with coal dust, people would ask: "Hey, Shaonian, are you going to somewhere?"

A good thing about being a fire keeper was that I had a different schedule from everyone else. Before the whole company woke up, I was already behind the stove in the pit, preparing the fire before the cooking team's arrival to cook breakfast. It would be dark and quiet in the warehouse. Down in the pit, I was alone. Actually most of the time, even with the commotion of the cooking squad in the front, I would be alone, down in the pit behind them. I loved it. To me the solitude was a form of freedom. Watching the fire dancing, the flame changing colors, from dark orange to bright almost brilliant white, the full spectrum of brilliant colors and hues were beautiful to watch through a small peeping hole, my mind would dance with them too, to faraway places.... I am a dreamer; even in school days, I could sit and dream in the class with my eyes wide open while the teacher was teaching.

By observing the fire and flames burning, I soon learned how to make fire burn strong when needed. The coal was rationed; with 200 people in our company, we were given a certain amount of coal for each month. If I used too much coal, by the end of the month, the company would not have coal to keep the stove going, which meant no cooked food for the company. Often I would poke through the ashes with a small stick to pick up small pieces of coal not completely burned. To make the coal burn efficiently, I wanted to redesign the stove, so that the airway was just right for the draft to go around the bottom of the giant wok. Eventually, my newly remodeled stove burned less coal because it burned more efficiently. The Headquarters of the Brigade sent male fire keepers from all other companies to come to learn my stove design.

When I was not busy, I would walk to the front to help the cooking team. Imagine cutting cabbage for 200 people for each meal. (Unlike in America's institutions or restaurants, the food is already prepared, bagged, ready to use.) We had to cut fast, as fast as a machine, with big choppers. That was how I learned to use a big chopper. I learned to cut vegetables without looking at the knife, so we could talk with each other and still keep cutting. I only had one scar on my fingers from an accidental cut. We made those steamed buns every day, and each one was rolled out by hand. To start, we would open 2 or 3 sacks of wheat flour (sometimes corn flour) and poured it onto a big table. The table was about one meter wide by two meters long. The flour was then shaped into a wide well, or a dam shape, with the four sides piled higher. Then we would pour wet yeast paste into the middle of the well. The head of the flour board - as we called the group who made things with flour "flour board" and the group who prepared vegetables "vegetable board" – the head of the flour board would give a command, "Ready, go!". All of us standing around the table would frantically push the flour into the center to mix with the runny yeast paste. It was just like construction site to mix a pile of cement with water and sand. You had to be fast to push back the runny mixture until the flour and runny yeast mixed well and became a solid lump, and no longer runny. Sometimes, if you were not fast enough, and the runny yeast with flour would breach down toward your side, it was like a breach of a dam. You would call out, "help!" But sometimes it would be no use. You would throw your whole body to the edge of the board trying to block the downpour of the running yeast and flour... down, down, the whole thing running down the board, down your apron, down your legs, on the floor. You became a flour figurine, standing helplessly, with arms stretched out on the sides. The sticky flour, yeast, and water mix would be dripping from your fingers, elbows, apron, knees. Even your shoes would be covered with sticky mixture. That meant we had to clean up the mess on the floor, and start again from scratch; open the flour sacks, pouring out flour, form a big well....

When no accident like this happened, after five minutes of frantically pushing, shoving the flour and runny yeast, we would have a huge dough mix. After it became a solid lump, there was no more danger of breaching, and we could relax mentally. Then we would start punching and boxing around the dough mixture. In that era, there were no mechanical or electrical devices in our kitchen, everything was done manually. The stove, the flour board, and the vegetable board; we definitely had our daily exercise. It was rare any one was sick, as our immune systems were constantly pumped up and going. Though we did not have much rich food, we were healthy. To knead the rough dough into a ready to use condition, we would stand around the flour board table and punch with our firmly gripped "mighty" fists into this huge loose lump of dough- left, right,- one punch all sides under the huge, solid dough. When the head of the flour board called, "one, two, three," we would lift the heavy dough and flip it over! Then, again, systematically, left fist, right fist, punch, punch. When the dough was ready, each of us would cut off a piece, about the size of a small pillow, and we would knead, fold, flip, knead, fold, flip. The movements became so in rhyme and in sync, that it was beautiful to watch the flour board people kneading, like a group dance, or martial art drill. That was the reason that as a fire keeper, I should have remained in the pit behind the stove, but I always managed to sneak to the front part of the kitchen to "help" knead the dough.

Being on a different schedule from all others gave me the freedom others would not have. I had to get up early before everyone else, so that I could start the fire, to have the stove ready for the cooking squad to come in to prepare breakfast. In the evening, after dinner, I would stay behind to cook food for the pigs. We raised pigs to provide meat for ourselves. The pig keeper, *Zhang Bingchen*, was from Inner Mongolia. He was probably the oldest young person in the company; he even had an unruly beard growing out around his chin! Everyone at the camp said that he was schizophrenic: they warned that when he was upset, he could kill! Everyone stayed away from pig man Zhang. I had to cook food for his pigs. We worked together for hours in the empty building, pushing the food around and around in the huge wok with a big shovel to keep it from burning at the bottom. During those hours, he would talk about philosophers like Hegel and Freud, things I never knew from my schooling. I realized that pig man Zhang was more knowledgeable than most of us young people at the camp. I was not afraid of him anymore; actually, I respected him for his knowledge.

There was no plumbing system in our living quarter section. However, the factory section had all the systems required for the paper mill, even though the living quarter section was only two hundreds yards from the factory, There was a small shed in the middle of our living quarters which served as a hot water distribution center. We all used thermal flasks to have hot water to drink or use in our rooms. When the whistle blew, we would line up in the shed to fill the hot water flasks. One day *Zhang Bingchen* came to the hot water shed, and while everyone was in line, he walked toward the front. People were afraid of him and simply let him have his way. He walked toward me in the front, took out an apple from his pocket, and handed it to me. Everyone was stunned: where and how did he get that apple? And how I could be a friend of his? People were whispering these mysteries behind my back.

I was a free oddball: I had my own schedule, and I was always covered with coal ash. One day, for whatever reason, *Zhang Bingchen* went berserk. He was running like a mad man in the woods behind the camp, screaming with a chopper in his hand. No one would dare to approach him, including the army authority. I was still at work that day when I was called to help the situation. When I got there, I simply walked to him and asked him to come back with me, and the situation ended peacefully.

The freedom from being on a different schedule gave me the opportunity of sneaking out of the camp sometimes. I heard that not far from our camp, there was a small reservoir, and I thought to myself, "Maybe I could swim there!" Even the thought of the possibility of swimming excited me. When I got a chance, I walked out behind the cafeteria building and through some small sand dunes, I saw a few wild horses and tried to get on one but was thrown off. It did not hurt, I simply rolled off the sand dune. I gave up the idea of riding a horse, though as a big city girl, it would be a thrill if I could do it. Maybe some other time. Right now I needed to investigate the reservoir. There was not a soul at the bank of the reservoir. The reservoir was not big but big enough for anyone to swim in. I took off my shoes and walked down into the water. The chill of the water made me shivered a little bit. However the elation of finding a place I could swim took over me, and the reservoir became my secret place. Whenever I got the chance, I would sneak out after cooking time, to roll down the sand dune and dip into the chilling water for a swim.

Chapter 9

Transportation Squad

It must be in early 1972 or 1973 after we started building paper mill at *Wanshuiquan*, and after working at cooking squad for a year, my secret visits to the nearby dam due to my unsupervised schedule as a fire keeper prompted *Lianbu* (company authority) to transfer me to the transportation squad, it was just established after we started the production line. The squad had about 14 members, half of them were young men, and the half young girls. Our task was to move all raw materials: coal, reed, caustic barrels of caustics, sacks of coarse salt, talc powder ... to the paper mill, and move the finished paper bales to the warehouse in Baotou, the nearby city.

Inner Mongolia in winter was cold, with open terrain, the cold current from Siberia blew freely through our paper mill site. There were two trucks assigned to work with the transportation squad, the drivers were from the headquarter of the brigade, not under the supervision of our company's authority. The trucks were Chinese made, sturdy arm trucks, with no top at the back, only high rails. With sub-zero Celsius temperature, we were issued sheepskin coats and fur hat like the Russians wear in winter. The short trip might take 30 minutes a long trip may take one hour. Our paper milled in the middle of no man's land, the road to the civilization was a dirt, bumpy road, we would huddled together in the open truck under a giant piece of canvas to ward off the Siberia chill. At that time China was a closed society, no boys or girls were supposed to be in body contact. As we all had to huddle together to stay warm on those open truck rides, the canvas was a symbolic wall, the division. Wang Jun-xiang, our squad leader, though he was one of us *Zhiqing* (school youth), was the first accepted into the company's communist party member group, would carefully arranged the canvas into two separate parts, girls huddling on one side, the boys huddling on the other side. *Wang Ju-xiang* came from Inner Mongolia, one of those local boys next door when we arrived in Inner Mongolia first night, one of those boys laughing behind the door. He got accepted into Communist Party through his hard work. When I was in No. 6 Girls High School, after I was accepted into Youth League, I had the ambition to go on to become a Communist party member, when I handed in my application, they told me that I was too young. I did grew and became "old". But in the camp, I lost my hope of being accepted to the party because of my "not obey the rules", because of my "not saying enough yes, sir", because of my "swimming in the dam". One day Wang pulled me aside and told me in low voice:" Last night at the Party member meeting, they were discussing you secret trip to the dam to swim, they will punish you next time if they catch you. Please stop this." I felt the sympathy in his tone, not as a stern criticize.

Working at transportation squad was not a light work, unlike the fancy name, it was not motorized work, all the material had to be manually transported onto the truck. A bale of finished paper was size of a chest drawer, about big poster size by compressed by 5000 sheets into a bale, it weighted like a ton, I am sure, now a days, it would be lifted by a forklift. In those days, there was no such a motorized devise at our camp. We learned to load the heavy paper bale by rolling it on long wooden planks rested one end on the bed of the truck, or walk a bale on its corners to maneuver it, it was always a team work, boys and girls, several pairs of hands to load one bale, then another, another, though hard, but seemed always filled with laughter. Because of the heavy work, the girls were allowed a day off when her period started, the other girls loved the privilege every month, I did not want it, I grew up more a tomboy, I even went to a photo studio one day to have a portrait taken, with hair hidden under an army cap pretending as a boy. Working with young men at the transportation squad, I did not want them to know I had period, so I would forfeit my one day privilege of not working. When we worked with course salt, a sack of salt would weight 200 *jin*, roughly 200 lbs, it was heavy, the young men would do the carrying of a sack on their backs, us girls only worked to lifted a sack to one's back. I wanted to be like the boys, I insisted to put the sack on my back, even though I was the smallest one among us. That was me, I wanted to be strong, to be the same as those boys. Many years later, one day a Chinese massage therapist was gasped when he saw my back, he asked if I had back ache, I said No. He told me that not often he saw people's spinal disks bulged out like mine. I told him that must be formed when I was working at transportation squad carrying heavy sacks on my back.

One day an order came that we must unload coal cars parked by the railway station nearby to clear the rail track. We were dispatched early morning, without break. Arrived at the railway station which was just tiny one room brick building, Wang Junxiang ordered one boy and one girl together unload one car of coal. One railway freight car of coal was probably several tons or more. All I could remember was that I shoveled, shovel, shoveled, I pushed hard with my body against the handle of the shovel into the loose coal pile, my arms were already too tired to push, then pulled out the shovel with coal in it, I had to lift the shovel and turn around, to flip the shovel to drop coal down the side of the car. My hands were so exhausted, they could not grasp the handle of the shovel firmly, often when I lifted the shovel, half way in the air, the handle would turn, dumped the coal on the floor instead of out to the side. Finally, I did not have the strength to lift the shovel, I started dragging the loaded shovel to the edge of the car to dump, though I had to walk extra steps, I did not have to lift the shovel. Wang Yang who was paired with me to unload the car, though he was the strongest and most masculine in our squad, was beat too, after several hours, all of us were still shoveling the coal, we were all exhausted, and hungry. Wang Yang, with each shoveling, he would say: "one mantou (steamed bun), just give me one mantou." We were not allowed to stop and return to the factory to eat until we empty all the coal cars and clear the rail track.

One day it was Chinese New Years Day, I overheard from *Lianbu* that there were 4 cars of reed by the small train station, they need to be unloaded, and clear the track. Hearing this, I wanted to save the rest of the squad from going out to work on the big holiday, I decided that I would do it myself. I walked all the way to the railway station, climbed over one car, started pushing and rolling down bales of reed, Children and adults from nearby village came out to see what was going on on the Chinese New Year's Day at the railway station, a small girl like an ant, on top of the freight car, kicking, pushing down the baled reeds, they shouted out to me: "why?" I told them that I would like the rest of the squad spend a restful holiday, they were moved, all of sudden, it seemed the whole village emerged on the railway, people including children, climbed up the ladders on the side of the freight cars, started pushing, rolling, before long, 4 cars of baled reeds were unloaded, my squad was spared from coming out on the Chinese New Year's Day.

When in winter season, the coal piles by the rail track were frozen into solid rock. It was not an easy work for us to move the coal to the factory. In warm temperature, we only need shovels to load the coal. But in winter, we carried picks, shovels. We had to chisel the frozen coal piles into small pieces, then load them. Soon we developed a method to move coal faster. We chiseled a big hole, at the lower part of the coal mount, it looked like a mini cave, then our girls would climb on top of the hill, "yi, er, san, flump!" we jumped together high with our knees bend, then landed with force on our feet, hoping with the collective force, we would knock down the ceiling of the coal cave we chiseled out. It worked, all of sudden, the ceiling collapsed, all of our girls tumbling down the slope, the young men waited below the slope would by instinct hold out their hands to catch the falling girls, then the last second when their hands were about to touch the girls, they would withdraw their hands, let us girls fall down right in front of them, because it was not allowed for boys and girls having any body contact.

One day we were working at the warehouse, I had to climb over to the rooftop on a long ladder, the roof was high, when I stepped on the last step, there distance between the step and the edge of the roof was still too big for a short girl like me to scale over, I looked up at the edge of the roof hopelessly, suddenly, a hand reached down, and it was Wang Yan, the strongest man in our squad, he said: "Give me your hand." I stretched out my arm, he grabbed my hand, and pulled me over the edge onto the roof. The moment he touched my hand, I was overwhelmed with the touch. It was the second human touch I could remember since I was a child. The first one, I remembered when I was about 5 years old, my father was giving me a bath in a big basin, I splashed water all over the floor, my father finally gave me a whack on my back, it was not a hard one, but I cried, my self-esteem was hurt. Growing up in a Communist society, particularly in my family, I did not have any human touch when I grew up, then going to a girls school, working at a camp. Now this contact with a young man's hand brought a tingling all over my body. I always remembered that first contact with another human being.

Young girls and boys working together under harsh condition brought us closer, one day, on the journey back to the factory, we girls curled together on one side of the truck, boys on the other side, I was leaning against the canvas, on the other side, it was Wang Junxiang, our squad leader, there, I was leaning right on top of his legs, there was only canvas between us, our bodies could feel each other, Wang did not want to move away from the feel of mine, he stayed there motionless, only bounce when the truck hit a bumpy spot, he was silent, though other boys and girls all engaged in talks. Finally, when the truck reached the factory, when we moved the canvas away, I saw it was Wang, at the other side of the canvas. Because of my weight on his legs during the long hour ride, his legs were totally sleep, he would not get up from the bed of the truck, all of us standing by the truck laughing and waiting for him to get up, though I did not say a word, I knew that Wang liked me a lot, the realization made me feel happy.

It depended on what we would move that day, if it was coal, by the end of the day, we were all covered with fine black coal dust, if it was talc powder, by the end of the day, we were all covered with fine white dust. We all wore same uniform, the girls all had same hair pigtail style, the boys all were same army caps. One day, while we finished the task at the warehouse in the city, we asked the driver to stop at a local photo studio, we pooled our money together and walk in the studio, we had a group photo taken 5X7. Two weeks later, we got our photos, one copy each as we ordered. But the driver revealed this to our company's authority, the following day, Wang Junxiang announced that *Lianbu* (authority) ordered all the photos had to be handed back and be destroyed, no boys and girls can be photographed together. Wang was admonished severely for allowing such activity to happen at all. We had to walk back to our dorm to get the photos before we departed for the day's task. When he finally collected the photos from each one of us, when he approached me, said: give me the photo." I shook my head, I said:" Tell *Lianbu* that I lost the photo." He said, "Wu Shao-nian, don't be foolish, hand back the photo." I said:" I lost it!" He said:" They will punish you." I said:"So be it." All the photos were collected, and handed to *Lianbu* (Office of the company). I was ready for the punishment, somehow, it never came. But soon after that incident, the girls squad was dissolved, from then on, only young men worked at transportation squad. All seven girls were resigned to different post at the production line. I was assigned to work at chemical Department. My job was to melt the caustic block in the steam bath. My sister Shao-hua was also ordered to work with me. Was it the result of the lost photo? There were 3 shifts, only our shift were me and Shao-hua, the rest shifts were boys. In our shift, we went to the storage yard to roll and kick in barrels of caustic rock. Once inside the workshop, we needed to open the metal barrel, and use sledge hammer to break a solid caustic rock into small pieces and push them into a steam on the floor, the heat of the steam would melt it into liquid form then pump it into other chemical solution to work with reed to make paper pulp. The work is dangerous, we were covered with thick canvas hood, face mask, thick rubber gloves, and rubber boots. The highly corrosive caustic would eat the skin right through if in direct contact. When broken down, the caustic had contact with air, it started sweat, became slimy, the floor of the work area became very slippery, when we kicked the broken down pieces into the steam bath, we had to be very careful, held a hand bar, so that we would not fall into the steam bath to be dissolved. We must have God on our side, during several years working at the paper mill, I had seen many accidents, young boys and girls, lost foot, finger, even life, I came out whole body physically. Any time when I recalled this period, I felt grateful to the universe.

Chapter 10

Zhiji (Paper Production Line)

In the old times, a paper mill needed water, nowadays, paper can be produced without water this was what I was told though I have not had the opportunity to visit a modern paper mill. To choose a location for a paper mill, the first condition is to check the water supply. The name of our paper mill location was called *Wanshuiquan* (Ten Thousands of Springs), definitely justified for the location of a paper mill, though there was no running spring on the ground, as a fact, the whole region was desert. But the aquifer below the ground must be ample, I wonder how the locals knew this without modern testing equipments.

The Paper Mill was quite a big factory, it had main building the size of 4 or 5 football fields put together, plus a few affiliated buildings like boiler section where there were huge furnaces to product steam, the steam was sent through big pipes to different workshops for different functions. Another big building was used as reed processing section, that building was built the first, formerly used as our makeshift cafeteria before the proper one was built. This reed processing building was the first building in the whole production line, beyond that, there was vast open field, hundreds of bales of reeds where piled up high, as high as 40 meters, looked like small group of pyramids with barren land and small sand dunes beyond that. To process the reeds, young men used big iron hooks to pick up the bale, flung it on to their shoulders, carried bales over their shoulders into this big building, then they loaded onto the conveyor, next person would use a big sickle to slash open the bail, the reeds was then feed into a cutting machine, reed stocks were cut into two inches long pieces, coming out at the other end of machine, another conveyer transported the cut reeds pieces up to the cooker ball which was on top of the building for the production line, it was the highest point in the plant. The cooker was as a giant cast steel sphere 5 meter diameter, it has a round opening of 1 meter diameter, the conveyer dropped the cut reed stalks into the sphere, when the sphere was filled with required reed stalks, the conveyer would stop, the chemicals of caustics nature were pumped into the cast iron sphere. The chemicals were used to breakdown the fiber of reeds. After the chemicals were added, the round lid on top of the sphere would be closed tight, with the push of a button, the giant sphere started rotating, mixing the reed and chemical, after some time, with turn of a big valve, the hot steam started pumped into the sphere, it was literally a giant pressure cooker, cooking the reed stocks into pulp stage. When required cooking finished, an siren would sound, that meant the sphere would stop rotation, the hot pressure needed to be released before the sphere could be opened. In old days, paper mills were notorious for releasing stinking sulfur smell gas into to air, the smell traveled miles away.... After more than twenty years, when I mentioned to Shao-hua that if possible, I would like to visit the paper mill for the old time sake, she told me, that the mill was closed long time ago due to its environmental hazards, now there were only dilapidated ghost buildings left there in the open land.

My sister Shao-hua and me worked at the Chemical section for several months, finally my sister Shao-hua was assigned to work at Shuxuan (Count and Select), the section where the paper was finally cut from big roller into standard poster size, checked, counted, and baled. I was assigned to work at Zhiji (Paper production line).

There were a few other small buildings for mechanics, warehouse, two rows of rooms for post office, management offices. A small building for as bath house after the shift. There was not running hot water at bath rooms. In the girl's bathroom, there were two shower heads with only cold water, a square bath size of 1.5 meter by 1.5 meter and 1 meter high made of cement, no tiles of finish it, simply a grey cement bath, there was a steam pipe dipped to the bottom of the bath. After a shift, when we needed a bath, we would filled the bath with cold water, and then walked to the boiler building to ask those young men to open the valve sending hot steam through pipes to the water in the bath. When the steam came out of the pipe at the bottom of the bath, the powerful steam produced loud sound, and sent huge air bubbles to the surface of the water, the whole bath looked like a giant soup pot, it only took a few minutes to get bath water heated up. Though primitive, we actually had Scandinavians style bath: in winter, we would turn on the cold shower head, soak the body with icy cold water for a couple of second, then jumped into the hot water bath, three or four of us would share the same batch of steamed bath. Sometimes, if the boiler section was under pressure of demand from production needs, or the coal in the furnace was not burning in full force, the young men there would tell us:" Sorry, no steam to your bath now." We had to wait, but sometimes we were too tired to wait, we simply dragged our feet back to the living quarter, hit the bed. *Wang Junxiang*, my former transportation squad leader, was then promoted to lead the boiler Section, we all worked on different shifts, we only met sometimes on the way to work, either he was off the shift walking back to the dorm or go to the shift. Wang was a quiet man, most times, he only smiled at me with his deep set piecing eyes. When we were on the same shift, the girls at my shift knew for sure that we could get a hot bath at the end of the shift, because *Wang junxiang* was on duty, if I walked to the boiler section, Wang would make sure that we got our water steamed fast, he often walked over from the boiler section to the bath building standing outside the bathroom calling out loudly asking if the water was heated all right. Other than these brief contacts with Wang, we never had any opportunity to be close again like when we worked, sweated, frozen side by side at transportation squad.

When I was assigned to Zhiji (paper production line), all my friends advised me to be very careful working on the line, there were frequent work accidents, young people would lose a finger, a foot... the production line, once started rolling, there was not stop, even with accident, you could not stop a line rolling, it would take many people at all the points to stop a production line. The line was about two meters wide, with many steel rollers, cylinders, moved by many gears, motors. When paper pulp was ready after treated with chlorine and other chemicals, it was pumped to a shallow pool at the beginning of the production line, a two meter wide woolen conveyer pick up the pulp, because of the coarse surface of the wool, the conveyer could pick up and carry the pulp through several presses to squeeze the water out of the pulp, the presses are made of hard rubber rollers, after going through presses, pulp was transformed into a continuous wide wet paper on the conveyor, the conveyer carried the wet paper rolling through the final drying press. The drying press was made of big stainless steel cylinder, with 1.5 meter diameter, when filled with high pressure steam, it worked like gigantic roller iron. When wet paper was fed through these steamed cylinders, the heat would finally dry the paper, paper would move out through the big hot ironing press, continued its final journey to a roller. The finished paper production at that point was a big paper roll, weighed several hundreds of kilos, waiting to be cut and selected and bales.

At any section of this production line, if problem occured, if the quality of the paper was not up to the inspection, the paper would not be allowed to roll onto the final roller. But you could not stop the production line from moving. If this happened, the production line was moving, the finished paper continued coming out of the final drying press, this paper would flow like a river, piled up at the end of the line, then workers had to move the sub-standard paper out of the way. The sub-standard paper would be parked at the far corner of the building, there was a small section to recycle the paper back to pulp. It was mainly a big cylinder, with rotating blade at the bottom, with water, to churn the paper back to pulp, pumped back to pulp tank.

Once the production line started, it rolled 24 hours a day, 7 days a week, two meter wide paper sheet kept rolling out of the line. My position at the line was to control the drying press. There were two production lines run side by side, they alternated, when one needed maintenance, the other could run. The two big drying cylinders were fitted one on top of another, the paper was fed in between them. My post was up the ladder to the second platform beside the drying cylinder. The platform was made of 50 cm wide wooden walk around rolling line, you had to be sure footed, not fall into the line, otherwise, it would be fatal. There were occasions, when some accidentally fell into the line, or just hand fed into the press, you would hear this screaming, then everyone at the line, would dash to the designated position for emergency stop, the line would be stopped, but injury was done. When I was assigned to the position, my friends were concerned because I appeared to be a tomboy, they worried that I was not careful enough, I could fall, I could have an accidence, and get hurt.

When I worked on night shift, I slept little in daytime. I felt it was a waste to sleep when there was sunshine outside, I would love to play outside for any reason. Then when night shift came, to fight the sleepiness, I worked out a plan: eat sunflower seeds. Most sunflower seeds in China were sold with shells on, at any social gatherings, you would find roasted sunflower seeds, so people nib on them while socializing . I filled my pocket with some sunflower seeds, once I got on the platform, my little corner beside those valves and dials, I would crack the shell of a sunflower seed between my teeth to keep me awake, it would be dangerous to fall asleep high up on the platform with all rollers moving. Each time when I fed the paper head into the rollers, I always reminded myself: "Careful! Feed the paper head, not your fingers." I folded the paper head with an angle so that the tip of the paper could be fed into the rollers, once the paper was "bit" the roller, I would immediately release my hands, so no accident of losing fingers. The noise of the production line was loud the moment when we stepped into the factory, afterward your got used to the loud "white noise", but it was still hard to communicate from my position high up on the second platform, we created our own sign language, when needed, we would blow a whistle, then signed with hands to indicate how dry the paper or how thick the paper, what they needed to adjust at the level below. With my second platform position, I could see the whole activities down around the workshop, all the way to *Shuxuan* (count & select) section, and all the way to the recycling corner at the far end.

One morning, when we walked to the factory for morning shift, we heard the news, that the night before the whole tank of bleached paper pulp was lost because the plug of the tank came off. One tank of paper pulp was a lot, the tank was two meter high with diameter of two meter. The authority issued the notice that it was a sabotage, someone pulled the plug. An investigation team from Brigade headquarter arrived, they took Zhao, the girl who worked at Bleach section on that night shift. Two days later, the investigation team announced that Zhao confessed that she committed sabotage. Now she was under the confinement, waiting for the police to come to take her away. In China at that time, such activity was a serious political crime, called *Fangeming* (anti-revolutionary), always was punished with prison terms. Though many years passed, I forgot many of my fellow young people working at the camp, I still remember her name *Zhao Minghui*, though we never worked together. I seldom even talked to her, but I remember her face clearly till this day. Zhao was always a quiet girl, always had a shy smile on her round face. Both of her parents were tortured to death by Red Guards during the Cultural Revolution, because they were *Fangeming* (anti-revolutionaries). The incidence of the bleach bank and Zhao's confession was a big event to our paper mill, we had a young *Fangeming*, she was only a teenager. Now she would be in prison, the police would come.... The following day, it was later afternoon, I was off, staying inside the dorm, then I heard the passing train suddenly screeching to a full stop just behind the compound, behind the woods, up on the railway embankment. "That was unusual," I thought, then I heard people's footsteps running outside, someone shouting: "Hurry, hurry, Zhao killed herself by lying down on the rail track!" "Go to see her body parts dragged all over the track!" My heart sank, I could not move one step, I did not want to see her bloody body parts, it was cruel. Mentally I shut my ears and my eyes, I did not want to be any part of this. My memory of Zhao Minhui ended with the train's screeching, with commotion of people shouting and running outside, then blank, I did not remember any of the end. Only her round face with quiet smile.

Months passed after that incidence. The shock of Zhao's suicide on all of us young people at the factory gradually subsided. One day, after previous night shift, I was just getting up in the early afternoon, the news spread at the dorm section: "Another sabotage event occurred on the night shift before." It was my shift! Someone found a piece of scale weights in the recycling cylinder, if the cylinder was started, the heavy cast iron weight would destroy the blades inside the cylinder. It turned out the weight was from the weighing scale beside the production line, the scale was to weight each finished roll of paper, to keep the record of each shift's production. An investigation team immediately arrived to our factory, since the weight was from the production line, all the night shift people were questioned. I remembered the night shift production: it did not go smoothly, the paper quality was substandard, so the paper was not rolled onto the roller, instead running out of the line continuously, it piled up, everywhere around the end of the line. I saw this ciaos from my platform up the second level, they needed help to move the rolled out paper away to the recycling section, to clear the space around the production line. I run down to help them, rolled up the paper, carry it on my shoulders, walked to the recycling section, drop the paper, and walked back and forth, with a few others from the shift. Finally we cleared the paper mountain at the end of the line, and with the adjustments made from other sections, the paper was tested up to the standard, it was running and rolled onto the roller, the production returned to normal. I returned to my post on the second platform. The rest of the shift was quiet, only the familiar white noise of the line running... This was my recall of the shift. "Yes, I was at the scene to help remove the paper to the recycling section." The investigation team jumped at my admission, one of them smacked down his palm down on the table firmly and shouted: "Tell us, why did you sabotage the recycling cylinder?" Another joined in: "We know that you hate the communist government." I replied: "I have not reason to hate the communist government, my father, my mother are all long time communist party members. You all know that I worked the hardest." The scenes of me digging at the irrigation ditch with sole of the shoes fell off, coal ash smeared face as a fire keeper in the pit, hunched back carrying 200 lb salt bag with the transportation squad, pushing reeds bales off railway cars on New Year's Day, hooded head, with big rubber boots, swinging the sledgehammer to break caustic rock....all this flashed through my mind, now they asked me why I hated the government! One of them shot right back at my hard work: " We know you worked hard, that is the way you vent your hatred for the government." "What a bizarre twist of thinking." I thought, but I could not win, they asked me to sign the confession, according to their verdict that I hated the government, that I put the weight into the paper rolled and carried it to the recycling cylinder, scheming to destroy the machine, and sabotage the factory.

After long hours of interrogating, after their firm pounding the table, stern shouting, the investigation team from the headquarter ordered me to be locked up in a room until I agree to sign the confession. I was finally left alone in a room, tired and frustrated, I tried to sleep, but my head felt exploding pain. I now understood how Zhou felt when she was investigated, and how she finally signed the confession paper. I did not want to end like Zhao. I wanted to live and tell. I decided that I needed to be healthy and strong if thrown to prison... finally I fell asleep. Waking up to the daylight, I jumped out of the bed. I looked out through the window, I did not see the guard assigned to stand by the door! I opened the door, dashed toward the woods behind the compound. Behind the woods, the slope rises up, there was the railway track.... I run and run, toward the woods, the guard reported to the leaders, they came out, when they run around the corner of the buildings and saw me in the woods, they froze there: there I was in the woods, doing push ups! They could not understand it, they though I went insane. They ordered me to return to the room. Three days passed, I did not sign the confession, the investigation team finally announced in front of the whole crowd that the investigation was concluded, that *Wu Shaonian* was at the scene of the crime. No further conclusion. *Wu Shaonian* was ordered to resume to work at her post temperately. The next day, when I put on my overall, walked in to the production line, I could see the sympathy in other's eyes, but no one dared saying anything, I climbed up to my platform on the second level, the moment my hands touched the handle of the valves, my eyes welled up, torrent of tears rolled down my face. Though I was tough with investigation team, I could not hide it anymore, inside I was broke feeling unjustified. The head of our shift standing below watched me, her eyes turned wet too, she had to walked away before others saw her.

Many months passed since the incidence, as life moved on, the plug of the bleach tank came loose again, the whole tank of bleached paper pulp was lost, this time, there was no *Zhao Minghui* there. There was no more witch hunt investigations. They had to replace the plug with a stronger one so that it would not be corroded.

Chapter 11

Shaohua, My Younger Sister

Shao-hua, my younger sister, went to Inner Mongolia with me together, though we were in the same company, we worked in different platoons except the period that we worked together at Chemical Section. Shaohua, unlike me, was more a conformist, peace maker, she never made any news in the company, she was talented in her own way, she was with company's propaganda troupe dancing and singing for a while. She was aware that her elder sister, me, often seen by others, especially by authority as a mischief. So most of the time, we were not together in our free time. I was more a loner, I liked to do my own things. One day, she came to see me, she said that she had enough of the life in the camp, she decided to leave the camp. I was surprised: that was a big decision, it took courage to defect the camp. Because in that era, everyone was confined by his or her registration by the government. If you were registered with camp, you could not survive at any other places, because everyone's food was rationed with coupon, each month a person received food coupons, which included: flour, rice. A family was issued along with a registration book, a food ration book, you could not buy any food in the restaurant or grocery store if you did not have coupon, money alone was not enough. That was how the government control the population. If Shaohua defected, even if she could manage to reach Beijing, which was 12 hours of express train ride away, how could she survive? My mother, my aunt, my brother, and younger sister Helen's ration collectively might support *Shaohua*'s food, but what about work, no registration, no work. There was no such thing like self-employed, or individual business at that time. That was against the law. Everyone belonged to a government unit. So I was really surprised by her guts to take this step, no one at the paper mill ever did this. No one ever talked about this. It was just unthinkable to our mind set of the Communist regime. It was like cross over Berlin Wall, suicidal!. But I could not change her decision. We discussed the best time for her to sneak away from the camp would be after midnight, when people were asleep, with darkness, people could not see her walking along the railway track. There was no boundary wall at our camp, it was situated in the middle of open desert. Shaohua needed to walk along the railway track for 7 miles to reach the train station of *Baotou* West, which would take her 2 hours in the dark. There she would hop on a East bond train hopefully to reach Beijing, the train stopped at Baoto West in the early morning 4 or 5 o'clock. She did not have the money to buy the train ticket. If she could get on the train and reach Beijing, how could she get out of the station without a ticket? I dared no think any scenarios. Sometimes in life, you had to resolve and do things.

The following evening Shaohua came to say goodbye to me, I wished her good luck. That night I laid in my bed, anticipating *Shaohua*'s defecting, counting the minutes, envisioned her small lonely figure walked along the railway track in the dark open desert...suddenly I saw people chasing her, grabbed her, I started screaming, then I woke up, it was my nightmare. The room was quiet, the camp was quiet, no commotions, no chasing. I fell asleep again.

I was woken by the unusual bugle blare, it was a tune for emergency! I jumped out of the bed, put on the clothes, run out of the room. There people were lining up according to their squad and platoon position. After we lined up in the formation, *Lianzhang*, the head of our company announced: "Last night, there was a defection occurred!" Whispers erupted: Who? Who had the guts..." "Silence!" *Lianzhang* raised his voice, "*Wu Shaonian*! Why did you not report to us of your sister's runaway?" The eyes of the whole crowd casted on me, even the lined formation around me seemed opened up, I felt I was in the middle of the circled crowd. I could not hide, I could not run, I had to act fast. I opened my palms, dropped my draw, I said loudly to the crowd more than to Lianzhang: "I had no idea at all of her runaway! My sister never told me anything." *Lianzhang* was furious, but powerless too. He finally dispersed the crowd, announcing that he would report the desertion to the headquarters immediately, and the government would do the search in Beijing and bring her back!

A few weeks passed, the talk of *Shaohua*'s desertion in the camp finally quiet down, then I got a letter from Beijing, from *Shaohua*, she was safe at home, government did not go there to take her away. She had food with family's ration, but she could not work. She hoped that somehow my father in Taiyuan could help her with a job at his company, after all he was in a high position of Government's big company. She never mentioned how she got on the train, how she evaded the checkpoint to get out of Beijing Railway station without a ticket.

****

It was August, 2002, one early morning at 3 o'clock, the phone rung in the living room, when I picked up the phone, it was my elder sister Qingnian on the other end from Beijing, China. She was sobbing, she delivered a bad news: Shaohua was hospitalized, the doctors' diagnose was very grim: she had brain tumor, it is astrocytoma, malignant tumor at stage 4, it was most aggressive brain cancer. The doctors' prediction for Shaohua: 3 months to live. The surgery was scheduled as soon as possible. After I put the phone down, my mind was racing. I was in Beijing two months ago with Shaohua, she complained of her low energy and shaking of her hands, she had been taking different types of drugs and radiation treatments from doctors to treat her hyperthyroid symptoms. Now finally the picture was clear: all the symptoms she had was from the tumor in her brain, not hyper-thyroid. I have been studying natural health since 1996. Through the extensive reading, I knew that I could offer some valuable information for Shaohua, but it had to be timely. Though I have many books and many video tapes on natural health, on several alternative cancer programs, they were all in English. To help my Shaohua, I need to put the information together in Chinese and in an easy to read form.

I am not a trained allopathic medical doctor, though I studied Chinese medicine, and acupuncture and finally got college degree in natural health. Most of my knowledge was required by self-education. To some people I could be a health-nut. It took me a couple of weeks to put the information together. I remember those days, while I was attending my health food store full time, meanwhile using every available minute write the paper in Chinese by long hand because I did not know how to use computer to write Chinese. As soon as one page finished, I would fax it to Beijing, hoping the information would inspire Shaohua, so that she would not believe the grim prediction of the doctors, but instead, have hope and not rush into chemotherapy. After *Shaohua*'s brain surgery, I sent the words to her: if she decides not to take chemotherapy, and get out of the hospital, I would fly to China to be with her, I would show her how she can regain health through proper lifestyle change.

On Oct. 17th I arrived at Beijing, as soon as I put down my luggage, I called American Consulate to ask of the process of taking Shaohua back with me to America, I knew if she could come to live with me for six month, the blue sky, green mountain and pure mountain air in Tennessee will nurture her back to health. I faxed 25 personal letters addressed to the ambassador. But as it was her fate, the American consulate refused to issue her a visa to come with me to US. I had to return to US without her.

In late Sep. 2004, I got news that *Shaohua*'s cancer condition returned, this time the location was at the base of her brain, where the spinal cord starts. The doctor's prognosis was very clear: death within 3 months. I did not want to accept this, even though I felt this is her destiny. In November 2004, I boarded on a plane to fly back to Beijing, my purpose of the trip was to convince Shaohua to do a total natural program, so that her life could be saved. I visited Shaohua the next day upon arrival, she mentioned that recently she did not get out to walk because her legs felt weak. To me it was the sign that the tumor was pressing the nerves. I mentioned that it's time for her to do my program seriously, she did not like it. She said that my program was too radical, all raw food did not work for her. Juicing was too much trouble. Plus detox was too much for her. I urged her to see a traditional Chinese medicine doctor... Shaohua called me when I returned to my elder sister's place where I was staying, she said: "Please, you do not need to see me in person. I felt pressure, and stressed when you talked to me. If you have anything to say, you can write it down, and drop it in the mail." So I did. The main point in my letter was to emphasis that she did not have much time to wait, she needs to take action immediately.

Two weeks later, Shaohua checked into the hospital. A couple of days later, she had operation. When I visited her in the hospital, she still had good spirit, she said when she gets well, we two sisters will have projects to work together. I smiled and told her that I look forward to that day. But deep in my heart, I felt this could be her last stay at the hospital, there might be no return for her if she depended on hospital treatments. I actually wrote her another letter before I went to see her. I started the letter with this line:

"Dear Shaohua, I hope that this is not the last letter I write to you. In my heart, I still have a hope of you recovery if only you listen to me, give my program a try. Due to your condition, only a radical program can save your life. That is to get out of hospital as soon as possible. Back to your own apartment, start fasting, drink only water and your own urine! Plus rubbing urine on your body, do this for a whole week. Please do not think this as a joke. There is not time to waste in your condition." I slip the letter under her pillow when I left her room.

Shaohua never mentioned my letter during my later visits to her, her condition deteriorated steadily. Two days before she died, when I visited her, I took bee propolis for her to take, though her husband watched me like a hawk. He did not like me to interfere with hospital's treatments. I felt that I was fighting a hopeless battle, her own husband did not like to see me with her at all. He felt that I was a troublemaker. He did not want Shaohua to go home. I told Shaohua that she might still have the chance if she quit forcing down all the junk food the hospital provided, and quit taking the medications the hospital gave to her. To convince her that urine therapy was not that nasty, I did unthinkable: in the presence of the nurse and her husband, I poured *Shaohua*'s urine from catheter bag into a cup, a full cup of her urine with all cancer cells, I drank it all. "Look", I held up the empty cup of her urine, "It is nothing! If I can drink Your urine, surely you can do it." She nodded her head. She uttered faintly the words: "Go and get mother, let her get me out of hospital." I promised Shaohua that I would bring our mother back tomorrow to take her home! But when I stepped out of her ward, *Shaohua*'s husband chased me down the elevator, he told me that in no chance that he would let her get out of hospital. We had a big argument in the lobby. By the time when I returned to Youth's apartment, I told mother about *Shaohua*'s request. That was like dropping a bomb into the family gathering. Till that moment all the family members hid the truth of *Shaohua*'s condition from mother, their reason was that our mother was 89-years-old, her health condition was not good, she could not take this. To me, mother is a wise strong woman, she deserves the right to know the truth and make her decisions. When I told her that Shaohua was dying in the hospital, that she asked mother to get her out of hospital, Mother said that she does not like the hospital anyway, even though she herself, a retired pharmacist worked in big hospital for many years. Mother told me a couple of years ago, she found a big lump in her breast, she did not go to hospital. She said, if she did, she would be long gong. Instead, she took some Chinese herbs, and massaging the lump daily. Now it's almost gone. My mother said that she would go to hospital next day, mother asked my other sister to arrange the car to go to hospital. I felt a glimpse of hope: maybe we could still save Shaohua with my program. The rest of the family was totally upset. They believed that Athenian would die, and let her die in the hospital. They did not have the resource to take care of her at home. So I had to see the rest of the family's stone faces for the remaining day. The next day was the Chinese New Year's Eve, the whole family was to have a banquet at a restaurant that evening. I was waiting for the car promised by one sister to take mother to the hospital. The car did not materialize until the dinner time. The whole family drove to the restaurant for the New Year's Eve banquet. After the banquet, the whole family went to Youth's apartment, playing mahjong with mother. I was in my room, it was already past 12:00 midnight, I laid in bed, I could not sleep, I thought of my promise to Shaohua ... the laughter from mahjong game drifted into my room, I cried silently, I felt helpless: all the years of my studying of natural health, I could not save my own sister's life. I was so close to her right here in Beijing only 3 bus stop's ride, but I felt she was like a hostage held up in a hospital beyond my reach.

I looked at the clock, it was 1:30 mid night, I got up. Put on my coat, I told the mahjong group, that I was going to the hospital to see Shaohua, one of them raised his head and said: "It's very late, there are no buses anymore." "I can walk to the hospital." I said and wondered to myself: my sisters' two cars parked outside the apartment, and he's talking to me of buses.... Luckily, I got a taxi on the way there. When I finally find my way to *Shaohua*'s ward, her husband was in the room, sleeping on a lounger at the far end of the room. The room was quiet, under the dim light, the monitoring machine showed her heart beat, blood pressure... it was not good, she was going, she was unconscious, mouth half open, with tubes all over her. I pulled a chair close to her bed, I held her hand in mine. Tears welled up in my eyes, I said to her: "Shaohua, if you have to go, please go in peace. Don't worry about the apartment, I will see to it that the apartment will be refurbished nicely." I told her that in next life around, I would like to be her sister again, we can continue the projects we planned to do together... I could not control my tears any more, I sobbed freely, I knew that she heard me, because when I spoke to her, the figures on monitors changed for better...

I left the hospital at 3:00 am. It was already the morning of Chinese New Year's Day! 7 hours later I would be on board a plane to fly back to America. My mother went to the airport to see me off, the other sisters promised my mother that on the way back from the airport, they would stop the car at the hospital so mother could see Shaohua.

24 hours later I arrived at home in Tennessee, I called my mother, She said that Shaohua died on New Year's Day morning at 5:00, two hours after I left hospital. My mother never had a chance to say good-bye to her daughter. This is my mother's regret till this day, even now when I talk to her on the phone, she would say," If only they let me know her illness earlier, I would nurture her back. It was the hospital that killed her." For me I felt it was *Shaohua*'s fate, she was

offered many chances or choices, but the bottom line was: it is her life, her decision, we could only share ideas, show ways. Although my sister Shaohua is gone, the revelation of the importance of personal responsibility is ever more clear to me. We are responsible to our life, not others.

Chapter 12

Arxiao

Though my sister Shaohua left the camp, I had another "sister" *Arxiao* with me in the camp. Arxiao was from Hangzhou, a city from the south. There is a saying in China, "*Shangyou tientang, xiayou Suhang*", which means there is heaven above, Suzhou and Hangzhou below. it equals the natural beauty of these two cities with Heaven. Naturally girls from Hangzhou were as beautiful as their city. Arxiao was the most beautiful girl among all the girls from Hangzhou in the paper mill. There were about two dozens of them assigned to our paper mill. They arrived after the paper mill was already in production in the mid 70's. They were at least 6 or 7 years younger than the first group. They were not "laosanjie" or lost generation as people in China now labels my generation. When we heard about new recruits coming from Hangzhou, there was eager anticipation among our "matriarchs".

Finally the day came, the truck arrived with them. Youth from Hangzhou added new trend into our *Laosanjie* group, they were from South, they did not go through Cultural Revolution, the culture influence was definitely different. Suddenly the monotone of our life in paper mill changed into vibrant colors. Hangzhou girls and even Hangzhou boys, wore colors, and patterns, their pants were tight, though at that time, we were not exposed to cowboys jeans yet. When *Lianzhang* announced the assignment of Hangzhou youth, Arxiao, the prettiest one was assigned to my shift, my squad and my room!

It did not take long before we two became inseparable. We were like twins. Arxiao wrote to her parents in Hangzhou, so when they had blouses made, it would be two pieces identical. we were about same height, we would wear same clothes, my trousers became tight too, I hand stitched the seams of the legs in. Arxiao was my shadow. In winter it was cold, we decided better to share the same bed to keep us warm. When taking bath, Arxiao would rub and scrub my back till the dead skin rolling off my back like many little worms. Now my secret trip to the reservoir was no longer a lone walk among the sand dunes. Arxiao, sometimes a couple of other Hangzhou girls would go there with me. Though she could not swim, she would watch me swimming. One day, we were hungry, we knew that not too far from the way to the reservoir, there was a patch of turnip field, planted by locals, but they always had watchful eyes from afar. We decided to take "a walk". We walked along the edge of the field, but dared not bending down to pull up the turnips from the ground, fearing the watchman afar would spot us, so we kept walking, but used our feet aiming the selected turnips, then we would gave it a good, fast kick, the turnip came off loose, then we would quickly pick up the turnip and stuff it into our pockets in seconds. Thus we avoided being caught by watch man. We walked to the reservoir, sitting by the bank, sunk our teeth into fresh turnips, hmmm, they tasted sweet and crisp like pears!

Many years past, though I would buy and cook turnips sometimes, I have not had any turnips tasted as sweet as those in the desert field.

One day somehow we had a bottle of Chinese wine in our hands! That evening, when no none around us, Arxiao and I opened the wine bottle in our small dorm room, the room was only a little bigger than a twin size bed (actually at that time, no one had the luxury of having a real bed, we upgraded from *kang*, the mud bed to wooden board, propped up with two work horses that you see at construction site). That was the bed we shared together, though small, but good to keep us warm in winter. The red wine tasted sweet, it was the first time I ever tasted alcohol. It was late in the evening, we did not have any other food to go with wine, but we enjoyed the illicit sweet nectar, the thought of our act of drinking wine in our little corner with no one around was more intoxicating than the wine. We felt a little sleepy, so we lied down and fell asleep. Suddenly, the emergency bugle blared up .... "Night drill!, Arxiao, get up and get ready!" I woke up Arxiao, jumped out of the bed. The room was in total dark. When there was a night drill, the power was always cut from the main switch board. We were trained to pack up our bedding stuff with a blind folder. There was always a packing rope under each *ruzi* (sleeping pad). I flung the packed bedding bundle onto my back, pulled open the door, dashed out. The cool desert night air hit my face .... All I could remembered of what happened afterwards was that I was drifting with endless ocean waves. When I woke up again, it was next morning. We lined up again in the open, with *Lianzhang* debriefing last night's emergency drill. *Lianzhang* called out loudly: "Wu Shaonian was heroic last night! Though she was serious sick, she participated the drill till she fainted!" Wow! That was the rare occasion that I was praised by *Lianzhang* In front of all others. *Arxiao* was standing next to me, she turned her head, our eyes met, only she knew the secret of my fainting sickness. Later Arxiao told that after I stepped out of the door I passed out flat. *Lianzhang* ordered two strong boys to pick me up, and put me onto a stretcher, those boys carried me on the stretcher and walked all the way through the night march in the desert that night. That was my memory of drifting with ocean waves. After that I dared not touch alcohol for a long time.

China lifted her Iron Curtain in late 70's after US president Nixon visited China. The political atmosphere changed from the top governmental level down to the grassroots. We could wear civilian clothes. With Hangzhou youth in the camp, we started to live a more civilian life. Before Hangzhou youth's in the camp, nobody ever received a package from home. We trained, we worked, we ate what was provided to us, we wore what gave to us. We lived an army camp life. Though there were no physical walls around the camp, the psychological wall built in our psyche was powerful, the brainwashing education we received through Cultural Revolution and the era before that trained us living like soldiers whether in an army camp or not. My little rebellions of studying English, swimming in the reservoir seemed defiant to authority in the camp. But Hangzhou youth it was different psyche, they did not go through Cultural Revolution, they did not remember the era before that. When they came to Inner Mongolia, it was boys Scout and girls Scout camp. Came with them, weekly arrival of packages from their parents in Hangzhou, food, snacks, latest trendy clothes. *Arxiao*'s parents sent blouses with pretty designs, and always in pairs. Arxiao and I would wear the same design. We were "twins" to others' eyes. One day we watched in a latest documentary news, U.S. president Nixon and his wife visited Great Wall! Mrs. Nixon wore a red overcoat on Great Wall. That was a powerful sight for us. Mrs. Nixon's brilliant red overcoat on top of the Great Wall was a liberation for our eyes and our mind. Soon after watching that news, *Arxiao* and I wore blouses made in brilliant red color with little black design on it.

To *Arxiao*, I was her role model. Not because I came from Beijing, or I came from a high ranking official's family, but my outlandish adventures of trekking through the sand dune to swim in the reservoir, studying English, producing handwritten novels for other youth to read in the camp, or taking pictures and developed and print them in my secret little lab. I even managed to have an photo enlarger made. So I had some rare photos of our life in the camp. I played volleyball well, I represented our regiment to compete in Beijing region army's badminton competition. Though I was branded by *Lianzhang* a university craze, a would-be- traitor of the country, to many of the youth in the camp, I had their sincere admiration.

The second year after Hangzhou youth came to the camp, we heard the news, the government had a new policy, the *laosanjie* generation were given the opportunity to go back to the school. Each unit would send two candidates for colleges. When I heard the news, my heart skipped a beat: "Maybe I can go to a university after all", I hoped secretly. But soon that hope was crashed. After the news of government's new policy, *Lianzhang* announced that the authority at the paper mill had selected two youth from us to go to study in universities, these chosen two were known apple polishers! From their selection, I realized I would have no chance for *Lianzhang* to select me to go to university, because I was not good at politics. Seeing those two packing and leaving the paper mill, I heart ached.

I continued my English study, even harder. I played less, when I had time, I would translate the novels. Then one day, *Lianzhang* announced the news: the authority appointed me and two others to start our own school. A new chapter of my life would start. Arxiao and I finally parted, no longer share the same tiny bed. I would soon move into new school built at the far end of the camp.

****

In 2002, I finally was able to go to China to visit after away from China for over 20 years. When I was in Beijing, I told Shaohua, that I wanted to visit the Paper Mill, she advised me not to go. The place was a ghost town. What about all the people worked there? "They eventually all returned to their home cities." as Shaohua told me. Where was Arxiao? She was from Hangzhou. I wrote a letter to *Hangzhou Daily*. I asked them to publish my letter to their classified ad, searching for *Arxiao*. Then I went to *Taishan* (Mount Tai), the No. 1 mountain in China. For many dynasties, the emperors held coronation on top of Mount Tai. Alice, my American lady who learned taichi with me, and I finally stepped up to the top of Mount Tai. While we walked along the street of Heaven, we entered the big bell tower. For each 10 yuan, you could strike the bell with big wooden plank, the plank was as long as two meters. Alice said that it was too commercial: to pay to strike the bell. I paid, I wanted to strike the bell, I wanted my bell sound to travel miles afar just like when we approached at the foot of the mountain, we heard the bell sound. I believed if my heart was sincere, it would transcend the commercial means. After the bell tower, we came to a Dao temple, with the drifting smoke of the incense and sound of bell, I felt the urge to go into the temple. But Alice said that she is a Christian, her husband is the head of the religion department at the college, she would not go into a Dao temple. "Come on, Alice, we traveled thousands of miles across the ocean, this is the opportunity to visit!" But her religion prevailed. I said: "Alice, I am going in! I don't care what kind of temple. God hears you at anywhere." Inside the temple, I chose one quiet hall, I knelt down, I made three wishes: *Shaohua*'s health, my return to visit China again, and reunion with Arxiao.

Alice and I did our Taichi and stick forms on Mount Tai. We walked all the way down Mount Tai, 6,000 stairs? When we finally returned to Beijing by train the next day, our legs were sore for days. But my spirit was not dampened at all: I got news from *Hangzhou Daily*, they found Arxiao. A week before I was returning to America, I got on a plane to Hangzhou. *Hangzhou Daily* arranged Arxiao to meet me at the airport. It was only an one hour and half flight, when I stepped off the plane, walked to the arrival gate, I looked eagerly for the reunion. 5 minutes passed, 10 minutes, 20 minutes passed, no one came forward to "claim" me. I paraded up and down in front of the waiting crowd behind the partition rope. All the people from my flight were gone. I started blaming myself for not even having a phone No. to call. I simply trusted *Hangzhou Daily* that they would be at the airport with a reporter and Arxiao. Finally, I approached one middle-age lady who apparently was waiting for someone for some time. I asked politely: " Excuse me, please, do you happened to be waiting for Shaonian?" Her face was startled, she cried out:" Are you Shaonian?", "Are you Arxiao?" I asked too. We both burst into tears. In the paper mill, we never shed any tears, all my memories with Arxiao were laughters. There at Hangzhou airport, we fell into each other's arms, cried and looked at each other, and cried in each other's arms again. We all changed, our youthful faces were replaced with middle-age plumped faces. No wonder we could not recognize each other even though I paraded in front of her for 20 minutes. Arxiao introduced her husband and their daughter to me. Then they took me to their humble apartment.

Both Arxiao and her husband left Inner Mongolia when the paper mill was shut down. They worked at another paper mill in *Hangzhou* until they retired. I stayed with Arxiao and her family for three days. We shared the bed again. Her husband slept in another room to give us maximum time to catch up with the lost time. The next day, we were all sitting in the room talking, Arxiao took out an old album book. The moment she took it out, Wang Hui, her daughter told me that for all these years, Arxiao often took out the old album, looked at those photos that I took and printed from my secret "lab", then she would feel sad. Finally Wang Hui told her mom put that old album away, because she did not want to see her mom feeling sad. Arxiao told me that a few days after *Wang Hui* told her to put the album away, one of her old friends from Inner Mongolia called her (most of Hangzhou youth returned to their city, they kept contacts with each other.) on the phone telling her: "Shaonian is looking for you." Arxiao did not believe her, she did not like people putting up this kind of pranks on her. She told her: "Go away." Then second person called her, telling her:"Shaonian is looking for you." She did not believe it, until the third person called her, told her to get a copy of *Hangzhou Daily*. Three days flew by. It was time for us to part again. But this time with modern technology, we're only a mouse click away, though Arxiao was not computer savvy, her daughter Wang Hui always keeps in touch with me. Last year, there was a reunion party at Hangzhou for people from Paper Mill, I wished I could attend, but I got a copy of the photo for reunion gathering, I could hardly recognize two or three from the group of thirty or more.

Chapter 13

School Teacher

Times changed. Even *Lianzhang* could bring his family from his village to live in the camp. Other shifu could bring their families to live in the camp. With their children in the camp, came the situation of children's education. An order came from the headquarter: Set up a school within the paper mill, so that children from all the families could receive education.

"Our paper mill should be self-sufficient," *Lianzhang* announced: "We have chosen three people to set up the school at the paper mill! They are: Yang, Liang and Wu Shao-nian." I was dumfounded. I was always criticized at the gathering, always a mischief. Now I was assigned to be a teacher! Both Yang and Liang were senior high school graduates, I understand for their role in setting up the school. But me, only junior high education?

Yang was assigned to be the principle, Liang and I were teachers. I would teach sports, music. The construction for the school started right away, within months, a row of rooms was completed, it situated at the other side of the paper plant, farther away from the production plant. I moved out of the living quarters for production people. I moved into newly completed school section. I had a room all just for myself, first time in life!

Several months after school opened, there was a fourth person joined the school. *Jin Su*, was transferred from other regiment to our paper mill, to work as a school teacher. She was a senior high graduate, she was from Beijing. She was from No. 6 Girls High School, though she was 3 years my senior!

Jin Su said that she remembered seeing me jogging along the small lane outside school in the mornings. She remembered me playing volleyball in the sports ground. We were from the same city, same school. As soon as we found out this odds, the mutual bond was formed. When Yang, the principle announced that *Jin Su* should move into my room, I did not mind giving up my newly obtained luxury of having my own room. With a role of a teacher, my trips to reservoir ceased, I still spent time with *Arxiao*, but with different schedules, different work, people at the paper mill no longer saw Arxiao and me together like twins. My friendship with *Jin Su* grew.

Jin Su was a big girl. Anywhere she went, she would stand out for her height and built. She was at least 6 foot tall, and weighted almost 200 lb. That was exceptional at that time, when China was not self-sufficient in feeding her people. People could be starving in rural villages. Now it is a national pride that China can feed her large population. Thanks to agricultural science research, the new hybrids, both rice and wheat, could yield many times more. *Jin Su* was big and tall, but not good looking at all. She had a big long face with small eyes, thin lips. She always wore a pair of glasses with dark rim on her face. When you saw her, she gave an air of coldness.

But with me, she would smile, we two would talk after the class in our room. She told me of her family in Beijing. Hers was a small family, only her mother, her brother. Their father passed away long time ago. Her mother worked as a manager in a neighborhood embroidery factory. They lived in a *hutong* (small lane) in downtown Beijing. Now most of those *hutongs* were gone, replaced by high riser apartment buildings.

Jin Su talked a lot of her brother *Jin Zheng*, apparently they were very close. She talked of *Jin Zheng*, unpopular with the factory authority where he was working. That struck accord with me because I was not popular with *Lianzhang* at paper mill. I considered myself a person always ready fighting for the underdogs. *Jin Su* told me of her brother *Jin Zheng* was unlucky in his love affair too, he had a girlfriend, who was from a higher position family. But in the end the girl ditched him. That evoked my sympathy too.

Our school days went fast, soon came the school's first summer break. *Jin Su* asked me to go back to Beijing together for the two weeks vacation. As a school teacher, naturally, you could only take vacation during school break. Each year we were allowed two weeks vacation back home city. I jumped at her suggestion, we went back to Beijing on the same train.

The next day I went to *Jin Su*'s place to meet her family. I bought a pair of tea mugs for *Jin Zheng*. Knowing his unlucky love affair, I thought the pair of tea mugs could bring him a good luck next round.

Jin's family lived in a small lane in the east side of Beijing. The entrance gate was traditional style, with 2 small stone carving standing of each side of the gate. The gate had a tiled roof top, high thick wooden threshold to step over. Once entering the first courtyard, there were several families living in there. On one side a path led into a second courtyard, there're a few families living there too. Another path on the side led to a third courtyard, a narrow one with a row of 4 rooms, 3 families living there.

Jin's family occupied the last two rooms in that narrow courtyard. They were small, about 4 by 6 meters. The floor was old grey bricks. The windows were traditional lattice style with glass replaced the rice paper. *Jin Su* and her mother shared one room, her brother *Jin Zheng* had his own room, the last one in the row, tucked back in the corner of the narrow courtyard.

There was no plumbing system in the whole court yard compound. Public toilet was outside the gate in the lane. There was one water faucet by the entrance of the gate, the water faucet came up from the raised stone platform, stood one meter high on the water pipe. Every family fetched their water supply from this faucet, or just doing their washing by the faucet on the stone platform.

In *Jin Su* and her mother's room, there was a double bed at the back of the room, a stove in the front of the room, a sewing machine on one side and a small table on the other side. There was a big water vat in the room for their daily water needs. *Jin Zheng*, being the only male in the family, took up the task of filling the vat regularly with a big bucket. It was a huge difference of living standard between my family and Jin's. My family lived in a spacious three bedroom apartment in the western suburbs. All people lived at our section worked for various government ministries. Our apartments were equipped with kitchen, bathroom, plumbing and central heating. In our three floor apartment building, there were six families, two on each floor. The men of all families were in higher level positions in the government ministries. In the mornings, each man would be waiting for his chauffeur to take him to work. At that time there was no private cars allowed.

But I did not see the difference on these. I had my experience with other girls in my class when I was in No. 6 Girls School, many of them living in downtown Beijing, living in small lanes. After living and working in the camp in Inner Mongolia, I was used to simply living conditions.

Jin Zheng had similar physical feature like *Jin Su*. He was tall with broad shoulders, same big long face, with small eyes. His eyebrows were strong, and they almost joined together in the middle between the eyes. He had same thin lips, but somehow they were put together in a positive way. His tall strong appearance was somehow handsome.

Jin Zheng even played violin sometimes. He was studying Japanese with one of his friends' mother. Studying Japanese! it struck accord with me because I was studying foreign language too, though English.

Jin Zheng volunteered to take us to places: Summer Palace, *Beihai* Park. In the two week vacation days in Beijing, I spent most time with *Jin Su* and her brother going to places, having dinner at their small bedroom/living room at the recess of the multi-family resided old court yard compound deep in a small lane near east side of downtown Beijing. My mother complained about my absence at home when visiting home.

The whirlwind two weeks vacation with *Jin Su* came to the end soon. I was having dinner with Jin's family that evening, the next day, we were going back to the school in Inner Mongolia. After dinner, *Jin Zheng* said that he would see me off at the bus stop. He walked me through the narrow lane, and emerged from the lane, we crossed the busy street to step on the sidewalk, the trolley bus Route 107 stop was right there. Route 107 traveled through downtown from east side all the way to the west side of Beijing. Now 25 years passed, though most of the small lanes are gone, I was surprised to see trolley bus Route 107 still running through the city, east to the west.

Jin Zhen proposed to marry me right at the bus stop of Route 107! Though I was not prepared to that, I did not object his proposal. He was the first man asking me, knowing his unlucky experience, I was ready to "save" him, my "fight for the underdog" spirit took charge, I accepted his proposal right at the bus stop generously. There was no romance in it, he asked me to marry to him, and I said yes. I felt that I was the shining saving knight, I granted the happiness to *Jin Zheng*: I was a good girl, surly I could make him happy.

When the bus came, I stepped onto the bus. During the long ride from east side to the west side, I sat alone in a seat in a corner of the bus, since it was late, not many people were on the bus anyway. I started pondering what I had just done. I lost in my thought, until the bus conductor lady walked to me and said: "Hay, girl, this is the terminal stop, get off the bus, we are going back to the depot!"

I woke up from my thought, realizing that I had already missed my bus stop. I jumped up to my feet, got off the bus. I had to ride another bus to travel back home.

I did not tell my mother that I accepted *Jin Zheng*'s marriage proposal until I was ready to leave for the railway station the next day. When I finally told my mother of *Jin Zhen*'s proposal and my decision, I could see the dismay on her face. She said: "They are very different from our family. They live in downtown small lane...." she did not say a lot, she knew her daughter Shao-nian, a headstrong girl. Once I made a decision, no one could change my mind.

I rode the bus to Jin's home first, *Jin Zheng* would see us off at the railway station. Before we left their compound, *Jin Zheng* asked me to go to his room. His room was even smaller than *Jin Su* and her mother's, a twin size bed, a small desk, not much space left. *Jin Zheng* sat on the edge of the bed, pulled me close to him. His face came close to mine, his lips touched mine, I froze by the touch of his lips,

I could smell his cigarette breath, I could see his closed eyes. Then I felt his hands came under my blouse, his hands touched my breasts, I could not move, I did not know what to do. I simply froze standing there like a statue.

Suddenly, I heard *Jin Su*'s calling from their room: "Hay, it is time to leave for the railway station." I jumped to my feet, and run out of *Jin Zhen*'s room.

Jin Zheng went to the railway station with *Jin Su* and me. The 10 hours of train journey back was easy, since most of the time it was in the night. Once we arrived at the school, back to our shared room, I told *Jin Su* of my acceptance of her brother *Jin Zheng*'s proposal, *Jin Su* jumped up with joy: " Oh, we will be sister in laws next year!"

The following day after I returned to the paper mill, I received a letter from *Wang Junxiang*. After I was assigned to work as a teacher at paper mill's school, after I moved to the far end of the paper mill, I seldom saw Wang any more. I eagerly opened the envelope. It was Wang's marriage proposal!

In his letter, he wrote: Ever since we worked and labored together in the transportation squad, I fell in love with you. But I had no courage to ask for your hand. You are like a ever-galloping horse, no one can rein you in…. Years passed, I could not hold this secret love in my heart any longer, I would like to marry you!"

My eyes became moist, I felt a skip in my heart, I wanted to rush to him, and tell him: Yes! Yes! Yes! I believed Wang's love, I felt his tenderness through his eyes when I was with him, but my tomboy nature did not let me think more than that. Now within 3 days, I had two marriage proposals!

But I already accepted one. I had to keep my words. I walked over to Wang's boiler section when he was on duty. They were busy, with shovels in their hands, throwing coal to the furnace, there was fire, steam, commotion, Wang spotted me standing by the entrance, he walked over to me, his face covered with coal dust and sweat, with his usual shy smile.

I pulled him aside, and told him that I read his letter, but I just accepted the marriage proposal a couple of days ago in Beijing. I said in a calm business manner.

It is fate, it is destiny, I said to myself. Had *Jin Zhang* not propose to me two days earlier, I knew I would accept *Wang Junxiang*'s marriage proposal. We worked and sweated together, I remembered his body lying against mine between that layer of canvas in the open truck on the bumpy desert road, I remembered how we laughed our heads off when he could not move his body because of laying there motionless for long time. I felt his tenderness toward me when he talked to me about my trips to reservoir. I knew he wanted to see me, when he walked all the way to the bathroom section to make sure we got hot water. Wang was a man of fewer words, but he has a set of piercing eyes, they were more eloquent than his tongue.

I did not want to see the hurt in *Wang Juxiang*'s eyes. I left in a hurry after delivered my statement: "I am going to marry to *Jin Zheng*, because he proposed before you, I accepted it, and I have to keep my words."

Chapter 14

Getting Married

Jin's family set the wedding date on next summer, when Jin Su and I could visit home when school was on summer break.

My father promised me that he would buy me a watch for the wedding. Wow! At that time, watch would be a luxury item and controlled by the government. even if you had enough money, you would need a permit issued by the government to be able to buy a watch from a shop. Each year, only a few permits were issued to a unit of workers. For us in the paper mill, I did not remember anyone was issued the permit. So to own a watch would be a really special privilege. The second luxury item needed a special permit from the government was bicycles. Beside the public transportation system, the mass private transportation was by bicycles, people often had to wait for years for his turn to be issued a bicycle permit. Some working unit adopted a lottery drawing method. You entered your name in the drawing pool, and wait for that lucky draw.

With the coming up wedding event, time went fast, the next summer arrived. Jin Su left the school before me to be with her family in Beijing to prepare for the wedding. After she left, I heard the exciting news: Anyone who wants to go to a university this year can put his name on the ballot. The government changed the policy toward the *Laosanjie* (old three graduates) generation regarding offering them a chance to go to university for their lost years during the cultural revolution. Instead of previous year of chosen by unit authority, we were offered democracy: put your name on the ballot, let people elect! Who gets the most vote, would be sent to a university!

This is my time, I said in my heart. After years of studying English, though brandished as a traitor of the country, as a university craze by authority, I felt that I had a chance with mass, many of them read my translated foreign stories, many of them liked to watch me playing volleyball games, they all heard *Lianzhang*'s frequent criticisms toward me, I had faith in their sympathy.

I wrote a letter to Jin Zheng at once to be posted to Beijing. In the letter, I wrote:

"Dear Jin Zheng,

This is a big news: this year, the government offered democracy election for anyone who wants to go to university. I want to give it a try. I will enter my name on the university ballot, maybe I have a chance to go to university.

If that happens, that will be a good thing for Jin's family. Think about it: I will be a university graduate, I will have a better career, your family will benefit at the end. Please remember that I will marry you as I promised!

If I go to a university, the wedding may be postponed till I finish the school, but the waiting will be worth it. I need time, I want to remain in Inner Mongolia until the election finishes. This is my chance. Please understand this. I will not go back to Beijing now."

The election went on as soon as the new policy was announced. It was organized in the evening, in the meeting room at the paper mill production site. All the young people gathered there, though not everyone was entitled to enter the ballot. You had to be a *laosanjie*, to enter the ballot. There were 6 names on the chalkboard. After the ballot tickets were collected, the crowd was waiting and watching from below, while *Lianzhang* and an assistant started counted the ballot verbally loud. I waited silently with the crowd, I heard my name called out: Wu Shaonian, Wu Shaonian, Wu Shaonian. When *Lianzhang* finished calling out the last ticket, there on the chalkboard, by my name, there were most *Zheng*. (Zheng is a character which was traditionally used as a counting unit, because *Zheng* has five strokes. It is easy to count how many *zheng*s to calculate the total number).

Lianzhang announced: "Wu Shaonian and another youth (I forgot his name after so many years passed.) would be presented over to the headquarter as the candidates for this year's university enrollment from our unit." The crowd could not refrain any more, they cheered with arms raised, they called out in unison: "Wu Shaonian! Wu Shaonian! Wu Shaonian!" After that rare election evening, Arxiao called it as American president election. She was so proud of me.

The euphoria of being elected by the mass to go to a university soon hit the ground. *Lianzhang* delivered the decision from the headquarter: "Wu *Shaonian*'s name was taken off the enrollment list. She is now on the waiting list, because her father's political status was not cleared yet."

Many high ranking government officials were in limbo during the Cultural Revolution, including the president of the country Liu Shaoqi. President Liu eventually died in prison. My heart sank, I felt it was the vindication from the authority, I was well-known rebellious to the headquarter officials, they probably still remembered the incidence of interrogating me for cast iron weight event. This was just their excuse to stop me.

"I am still on the waiting list, that means if anyone else was disqualified, I will be back on the list. I came so close to my dream, I should wait!" I did not want to give up, this was what I kept telling myself.

I was waiting for the miracle to happen, waiting for the next news from the headquarter. The next day, Arxiao was with me in my room, since the school was already closed, I was just waiting for the final outcome of university enrolment, it was so close, I knew it would be just days to know the final outcome. Suddenly Jin Su burst into the room. Her big long face was now even longer. She said: "Why are you still here? The election was over, your name is off the list!"

I said: "It is not over, my name is on the waiting list..." before I could finish the sentence, I felt a big whack on my cheek, Jin Su slapped me: "We are all waiting for you coming back to Beijing for the wedding!" I was dumbfounded. I never received physical insult like this before. I grew up in a well-mannered family, my parents all talk quietly, never heard any curse words, not to say this physical insult.

"OK," I said, "I will return to Beijing tomorrow. I thought that if I can go to university, your whole family will benefit, since you all don't care for this, I keep my words, I will marry to your brother and give up my university chance."

Arxiao begged me, "Don't! Shaonian, you came so close, you wanted university, wait for a few more days!"

I was a noble knight, I could sacrifice my university, just to keep my words: I would marry to Jin Zheng. I got on the train the next day with Jin Su.

Jin's family did not have much to prepare for the wedding, there was not much space in Jin Zheng's room to put much furniture, he changed his twin size bed to a double size bed. My father promised me that after the wedding, he would have a wardrobe made and a small table to fit into that tiny room. Jin's mother provided us two silk brocade quilts as the tradition for the news weds.

The wedding ceremony was simple. Only my mother came to the ceremony. Jin's family had two tables set up in their narrow courtyard. They cooked some dishes. Jin's family relatives were few, only their aunt and her husband, Jin's best friend Liu, who's mother was teaching Jin Zheng Japanese. There was some wine at the table, I saw my mother wiping tears from her eyes while sitting by the table quietly. People say that was normal, the mother of the bride often cry. I don't remember what kind of clothes I was wearing. The event was so insignificant to me. I was simply fulfilling my words, to grant happiness to Jin Zheng as I thought I could. The only memory of the wedding ceremony was my mother's tears.

There was no wedding night anticipation for me either. The previous day when I returned from Inner Mongolia, Jin Zheng took me to his room. He started with kissing my lips, then progressed to laying his hands on my breasts, then he was on top of me... my pants was pulled down, my underwear was pulled down. When he pushed himself inside me, I groaned with pain. After that he said that I did not bleed, maybe it was because I was athletic. I did not understand what he meant. I remembered the pain each time when I went to the toilet to pee.

So I was married, I became a member of Jin's family. They clearly made me understood that I should stay at home in their two small rooms at the recess of the big courtyard compound deep in a small lane in downtown Beijing.

One day after the wedding, I was playing badminton with someone outside on the street of the small lane, Jin Zheng's mother called me, she pulled me back to the room, and told me that I was a married woman, it was not appropriate to play sports on the street. She said that she would teach me to do the right thing for a married woman. Sewing. There was a sewing machine in the room. Though she passed away many years ago from cancer, there is one thing that I felt in debt to Jin Zheng's mother, that is the sewing skill. The skill proved useful till this day. Even now with my studio, I often mend students tore pants and uniforms.

Two weeks of wedding/honeymoon soon ended. I would travel back to Inner Mongolia to start my school teaching with Jin Su the next day. The night came, I went to bed with Jin Zheng. To perform my duty of a wife, I was laying there letting him push himself inside me. Then he discovered that my period started, I was bleeding, when he saw the blood of me, he was dismayed. This was his last night with me since I was leaving tomorrow. He got so annoyed for the timing of my menstruation, he kicked me out of the bed, and pushed me out of the room and locked the door behind of me.

I stood outside the room against the wall. It was late. The light from Jin Su and her mother's room was out, they must be asleep. I did not want to disturb them anyway. I did not want to walk away, where? My mother's place? It was a long bus ride at the other side of the city. I did not want to see my mother crying for me ever again after seeing her at the wedding.

I stood there under the overhang of the roof. Luckily it was in summer, not cold, I looked up at the moon, the reality hit me as clear as the clear night sky: this is my wedding, this is my honeymoon. It is done.

Once back to the school in Inner Mongolia, I was one of the very few, a married woman. Arxiao came to me, she told me that a few days after I left the paper mill, the headquarter did send for me to be back on the list to go to university. I did not blame anyone. I didn't even tell my family. It is fate, it is destiny, I said to myself. I made the decision, I shoulder the consequences.

Wang Junxiang came to see us too as many other friends at the paper mill. But he came back again and again. Soon the rumor in the paper mill was that Wang *Junxiang* and *Jin Su* were dating! That was a big shock to all of us. *Wang Junxiang* was three years younger than *Jin Su*, plus Jin Su was big, she was ugly according to traditional Chinese standard. Wang was young, good looking, good position in the paper mill, he could choose many other pretty girls. Wang started coming to our room almost every day, *Jin Su* was all smile, proud that she had a boyfriend.

One day when Jin Su hurried to her class, *Wang* was left in the room with me. I asked him: "Why! *Wang*, Why did you date with Jin Su? She is ugly, she is not sweet! She is older than you." Looking straight into my eyes, *Wang* said: "It is for you. If I can not be your husband, at least I can marry *Jin Su*, so that I will be a member of the family, so that I can be near to you, I can see you often!"

His words broke my heart, my eyes filled with tears. What have I done? I married to a man, who was so hard hearted cold to me. And I broke a man who was so sweet to me.

Wang saw the tears in my eyes, he pulled me close to him, he started caressing me, I did not want to resist him, I hurt him enough by marrying to Jin Zheng, I could not stand to hurt him further by pushing him away.

Jin Su and *Wang Junxiang*'s dating continued, they were talking of marriage. Time went, the following summer break time. Again, the government changed the policy toward *Laosanjie* group, that year anyone who was *Laosanjie* could apply for university, if he or she could sit in for the entry exam and pass. Both Jin Su and I applied for the entry exam. Jin Su passed the exam, I failed at mathematics, I only had junior high schooling, I had not studied calculus yet. So as the fate, that summer, Jin Su passed the university entry exam for *Laosanjie* group, the last chance from the government granted to *Laosanjie*. She was assigned to Beijing Finance College, she packed her belongs, said goodbye to Wang Junxiang, left for good. I returned to Beijing too, as a wife of Jin Zheng.

Gone were the days of my free spirited tomboy. Now I was a housewife in Jin's family. Early in the morning, I would jump out of the bed, hurried to prepare breakfast for Jin Zheng, Jin Su and their mother. One morning I was busy getting the breakfast ready, Jin Zheng stepped beside me, he asked me:"Have you washed your hands this morning?" I paused, I shook my head, "No."

"Throw this food away. Wash your hands, and cook a new batch!" Jin Zheng ordered. I said nothing. I was not a quarrelsome girl, I hated people arguing. Though I did not say a word, I did not like Jin's family, they were cold-hearted bunch. I cooked another batch breakfast for them.

Though I was back in Beijing for vacation, Jin Zheng did not want me to go back to my mother's place to visit, staying overnight at my mother's was unthinkable. I spent all my vacation time cooking for them, learning sewing, embroidery. No more parks to visit as my first visit with his family. He mentioned that I was too short, he did not want to walk together with me. We only had one photo taken together at a studio for the wedding. When we got divorced, Jin Zheng cut it up. I did not have a single photo of him.

I was looking forward to return to Inner Mongolia. In the big sky country there I could be myself again, my free spirit could return to me. After returning to Inner Mongolia, Jin Su was not there anymore. She was in college in Beijing. I had my room all by myself again.

Since Jin Su left the paper mill, Wang got a new girlfriend Liang, she was also tall, but slim, pretty. Liang was the nurse at our little emergency room. Everyone at the paper mill knew their dating, because they were always together, they looked a perfect couple. They even had a trunk made. At that time in the paper mill, if you got married, you would have a wooden trunk, which you can keep two people's clothes in it, and put two bed boards together to form a double bed. That was marriage, no ceremonies. So seeing them having a trunk made, that meant they were going to get married soon!

But Wang's fate turned downward again. Before their planned marriage, Liang was transferred to the clinic at headquarter, which was 15 miles away in the mountain. Since Jin Su left the paper mill, Wang no longer visited our room, he was happy with Liang.

Then one evening, there was a knock at my door, I opened the door, there was Wang standing there, I let him in. I was surprised seeing him. He sat down in a chair by the window near the door, with his head down.

"What's matter, Wang?" I asked. He raised his head, I could see tears in his eyes. "Liang called off our wedding." he said in a low voice.

"So soon." I commented. Liang left the paper mill not longer than two weeks. Wang was obviously heart broken, his head was down again, his body was shaking, maybe he was sobbing? it was hard to see him broken like this. I reached out to him, my hands patted on his back, then I found we're in each others arms. There was no caressing, only holding. Later he left the room.

That was the beginning that Wang started seeing me again. Often after school, in the evenings, Wang would stop by my room. Wang was a quiet man, when he came to my room, he would sit in the chair by the window content. I would be busy doing my own things, cleaning, preparing food, reading... We didn't talk a lot. He was content just being there with me , watching me doing my things. There was physical caressing with each other. We were like old married couple, content with each other's company.

Then one evening, I said, "Hay, Wang, it is getting late, I need to sleep. You should leave." Wang smiled, but he did not move. After telling him several times that he should leave, I could see that he wanted to stay. As a married woman, I realized if he stayed in that room that night, he would be in my bed, and sex would be inevitable. I decided that I wanted to give him myself, this would be my ultimate gift to Wang as a return for his love for me.

I locked the door. Turn off the light. I took off my clothes, laid down in bed, and asked *Wang* to join me in bed. Wang was gentle with me, I did not have any pain. But I did not have any memory of intimacy. I laid there to offer myself to Wang as a return for his love for me. He made love to me, later he left.

The next morning, when I woke up, I realized that I committed adultery, a crime more grime than a political offence. The following evening, there was the usual gentle knock at the door, I knew it was Wang. I did not open the door, I called out through the door: "Go away. Wang, I did not want to see you anymore." I blamed on him, because of him, now I am a sinner, the worst kind in the world. Now I could no longer hold my head high, because I knew I committed adultery. I always regarded myself noble, now, an angel had fallen.

As history played out its irony, later, *Lianzhang* was caught while he was having sex with one girl who was the head of one platoon.

At that time, we did not have any refrigeration system. In winter time, we store all root vegetables (potato, carrots, onions, Chinese cabbages) in huge cellars we built. The cellars were dug deep in the ground, they were big inside, with 10 by 30 feet wide, 6 feet high, supported by thick strong wooden pillars. The cellars were closed with roof, and on top of the roof there was 3 feet thick dirt. It could be sub zero freezing cold in winter, or very hot in summer, once inside the cellar, the temperature was always same, pleasant.

The apple polisher platoon head, the girl, and *Lianzhang* sneaked into a cellar, someone saw the pair, he alerted others, when the crowd went into the cellar with flash light, *Lianzhang* was caught with his pants down, laying on top of the naked girl. That was a big scandal. The news traveled fast to the headquarters. The girl's family members, father and uncle, appeared in the paper mill one day. They found out where *Lianzhang*'s house was, they went in, and gave a good beating of *Lianzhang* in front of his wife and children. After the beating, the family demanded that the girl to be released from the camp to return to Beijing. The headquarters granted their demand to quiet down the scandal. That was a good trade off for the apple polisher platoon head. She had sex, and had the privilege of leaving the camp.

Chapter 15

Longlong, My Son

Summer 1976 I left the school a month before the summer break to travel to Beijing, my pregnancy was almost over. I arrived in Beijing, the next day I went to a hospital near Jin's home. The result of check up was good, everything was normal. It was just a matter of waiting for the due day.

Jin's family decided to upgrade their living condition, they would replace the old grey brick on the floor with cement, and to build a small kitchen shed outside opposite Jin Zheng's little room. Since it was a narrow courtyard, the division wall was 5 meters from Jin Zheng's room. They decided to use that wall as the support, and build a shed 1 by 2 meters, so that they could move the cast iron stove from Jin Su's and her mother's room out. The cooking could be moved outside to the shed.

It was major upgrade. Jin Zheng said that he could get some cement for the floor through his friends. But for the shed, we would need some bricks, though it would be a small shed. Where to get bricks? At that time, no individual could purchase building material. I walked around near their area, I discovered a construction site, there were always some loose bricks laying around. I started making trips to the site. Each time, I would carry one piece of brick in my hands back, no one would stop a pregnant woman picking up one brick.

It did not take long, there was a stash of bricks piled up at the corner of the narrow courtyard. Jin Zheng announced that there was enough bricks, the "construction" of our new floor and kitchen would start that weekend. Liu, his friend would come to help with construction.

The building work started early on Saturday. I wanted to help, even with my heavy belly near the end of the pregnancy. I held the shovel firmly with my hands, mixing sand and cement, it brought back the sweet and bitter memory of shoving coal in transportation squad. I swung the shovel high, up to the roof of our new kitchen shed. I was a pro at swing the shovel with heavy cement mix, I felt proud at that moment, that was the rare moment that I felt we were the family: Jin Zheng, Jin Su and their mother.

The "construction" work took the whole day, Jin Su and her mother took up the cooking task. There was good food, even beer for Jin Zheng and his best friend Liu. There was laughter by the table, the rare moment to see Jin's family laugh. It was so satisfying to see the smooth cement floor and a kitchen, a real kitchen standing on the other side of the courtyard 5 meters away.

Liu said goodbye and left. We soon retired to our rooms, and fell asleep from exhaustion. Early in the morning, the cramping in my belly woke me up, it went on and off, I woke up Jin Zheng. "Jin Zheng," I said, "I think it is time now, please hurry up and take me to the hospital!"

It was almost 5 o'clock, the small lane was quiet, there were few people on the street. Jing helped me to get onto the back of his bicycle. It did not take long for us to arrived at the hospital.

The nurse at the Birth Delivery Section checked on me, and told me to go home. She said I was early. But I did not want to go back home, I sat in a chair outside the Delivery section. Within one hour, my water broke, when I went into the deliver section, the nurse had to call for help to wheel me into the delivery room immediately.

There were two delivery tables in the room, the only doctor in duty was working with one woman in labor. They put me on another table, I could not hold any more, the baby was coming out! The doctor at the other table told nurse to push my baby back! Because he worked on the other lady. So the nurse used a big piece of cloth folded as a pad to push the baby from coming out. She kept telling me: "Don't push. Don't push. Say: Haaa.... Haaa..."

Finally the doctor run over to me, he discovered that it was not baby's head that the nurse was pushing, it was baby's buttocks! It was a boy. The length tug war battle between the nurse's pad and the baby's tender buttocks bruised his little tender testicles, that left permanent marks on his testicles.

So was my son's arrival to the world, I think the vigorous swinging of shovels of mixed cement expedited the delivery. I did not have much pain as many women experienced.

We named our baby *Dalong*, which means Big Dragon, since 1976 was the year of dragon. We called him *Longlong* as his pet name.

With the arrival of *Longlong*, my relationship with my mother-in-law deteriorated. I had to juggle between feeding and taking care of the baby and taking care of Jin's family. To be able to sleep 8 hours undisrupted was the only wish I had in the whole world. One morning while laying in bed to cherish the rare moment of sleeping, Longlong was not up early as usual, I heard the calling from Jin's mother: "Help, Help." I got up, running over to her room, there she was laying in bed, saying: "I'm not well, and you are not here to check on me." Then she pointed to her night pot: "Take this out, and empty it!"

I felted insulted, I could see that she was perfectly all right. This was her way to belittle me to show that she was in control. From that day, I seldom spoke to her, and no eye contact either. Living with Jin's family was unbearable. But I had my son from Jin Zheng. I had to look after the baby. He was so vulnerable, I wanted to nurture him with my breasts as long as I could, even I had to empty Jin's mother's urine pot every morning.

One month passed after *Longlong*'s birthday, one morning, I had been dreaming of thousands of horses and chariots galloping on the Mongolia desert, the rumbling was so powerful, even my body shook… suddenly I woke up. I could feel the rattling of the windows. I could feel the movement of the bed. "Earthquake!" With flash realization, I grabbed Longlong beside me, started pushing Jin Zheng on the other side of the bed, "Wake up! Wake up! Jin Zheng, it's earthquake!"

I dashed out of the room with *Longlong* under my arms, before I could reach the small corridor door which led to the middle courtyard, it collapsed. I stepped over the debris of the collapsed gate, proceeded to the front gate.

Once on the street of the small lane, there were people everywhere. It was around 5 o'clock in the morning, most of people were still in bed when quake struck. Most people on the street were in underwear, pajamas, or half naked. I saw Jin Zheng's mother, seeing her mother standing there on the street in her underwear, I chuckled inside me. When I looked down to check Longlong, I realized that I had been holding him upside down all this time. He did not wake up!

By 7 o'clock, from the radio news, we heard that there was a big earthquake, the epicenter was at Tangshan city, it was about 120 miles from Beijing. The quake was so powerful, that 250,000 people perished. The order came from municipality, people living in old courtyards in downtown were not allowed to live inside their rooms. Overnight the streets in downtown Beijing became a tent city.

Nursing a one month old baby in a makeshift tent on the street was not easy. Jin Zheng's mother agreed to let me take the baby and travel to Taiyuan, the city where my father was living and working. My aunt Baibai travelled with me to help with a baby for the train journey.

All the trains leaving Beijing were full, tens of thousands of people were travelling outside Beijing to avoid living in a tent on the street. We were lucky to have one seat, I let my aunt to sit in the seat, she was over 70's. I managed to sit on the little table by the window between the seats . The table was high, I my feet dangling from the edge of the table. I had to raise my arm up to hold on to the luggage rail above my head to keep me from falling, while the train swung from side to side. I even managed to hold *Longlong* in one arm, and held the overhead rail by another arm, and fell asleep, without loosing Longlong or fell of the table!

My father and his driver were waiting for us at the railway station. Once in the car, my father told me that he cooked a big pot of chicken soup with red jujube dates and other herbs. That would nurture me and the baby after the ordeal of birth and earthquake.

It was almost 10 o'clock in the morning when we stepped into my father's apartment. It was huge comparing to Jin's family's two rooms. There are five big rooms connected with foyers, and corridors. Actually his apartment was two apartment units connected together.

Each room was twice the size with Jin Zheng and his mother's rooms combined. There were three balconies. There are many flower pots on the balconies, some of them with full bright flower blooms. My father had a hobby of growing plants, and flowers, they were indoor and outdoors on the balconies.

I was tired from the train ride. As soon as I finished chicken soup, I felt sleepy, my aunt urged me to lie down to rest, she said that she would look after Longlong. The touch of the soft bed, the smell of the newly washed sheet … I drifted into my sleep. When I woke up, the room was quiet, I walked into my aunt's room, she was asleep with *Longlong* sleeping by her side.

My father must have left to his office. My elder sister Qingnian and her son, Jiajia, who was 5 years old at the time, were living with my father. They were not back from work and school yet. I quietly closed the door of my aunt *Baibai*'s room. It was around 4 o'clock. I had slept un-disrupted for long hours since Longlong was born. No calling from Jin's mother asking to empty her urine pot. I felt good, moved away from psychological bullies like Jin's family, I felt life energy came back to me.

I heard some unusual sound coming from my father's side of the apartment, so I walked along the long corridor that led to my father's room. There was a large foyer at the end of the corridor, at the other side of the foyer there was my father's room. It was in another part of the apartment.

When I pushed open the door of the room where the sound came from. I saw a tall young man hovering over a wooden plank. He turned around when he heard me opening the door, with a plane in his hands. With a smile on his face, he introduced himself: "Hi, there, I'm Xiao Lin. You must be Shaonian. Your father asked me to make some furniture for him."

Lin was his family name. In China, it is a common practice to call younger people with Xiao and family name, Xiao Lin meant Junior Lin. Lin was a carpenter working for my father's company.

Suddenly I heard a faint cry of *Longlong* from the other side of the apartment. I hurried over, when I came back to Lin's "carpentry shop", I had *Longlong* in my arms. My father converted his big bedroom into a workshop for Lin. He moved into the sun room next to his bed room. He did not mind sleeping with his plants.

I sat down in a chair in the room, there were a couple of finished furniture in the room, they looked beautiful with refined lines and finish. I could see Lin was skillful. He looked at me and Longlong, and said that he had a young son too, who was 3 years old. We started talking while he was working on the plank. Soon it became a routine for us: I held *Longlong* in my arms, Lin worked on his furniture, and we talked, talked.

I felt like a princess at my father's place. I was his favorite child. With my arrival, my father rolled up his sleeves, outshined his culinary skills. The stove top in the kitchen always had several black glazed clay pots on it. He definitely inherited my ground-father *Clay Pot Wu* in the spirit! He took great prize in his black glazed clay pots, they came in different sizes, he always kept them clean and shining on the shelves when they were not on the stove top. My father cooked all kinds of soups, which he said were the best for a nursing mother.

One day in Lin's "workshop", he asked me jokingly; "Why do you always wear old women's clothes?" Looking down at my cotton top, which was Jin Zheng's mother's hand-me-downs, it was in traditional style, knotted buttons were on the side of the jacket. Only grannies in bond feet wore those style at the time. I told him about my mother-in-law. I could see from his eyes he became quite sympathetic.

He told me that he was lucky, after marriage, they lived with his wife's family. At that time, most young married couples did not have their own housing. Jin Zheng, who had his own room, no matter how poor standard, was considered by many a lucky one. Lin said his mother-in-laws were very kind to him.

Lin did not go back to his family everyday, because they lived quite far outside the city. He went back to visit them on weekends. He slept in one of the rooms at my father's room section.

One day Lin asked me why I was different from other people, not only I wore old women's clothes, but I also studied English, he said he never saw anyone studying English. It was odd. "It is my hobby just like a hobby of my father's: growing plant, cooking." I said, "A hobby keeps one alive, give one an identity."

I then asked Lin: "Do you have a hobby beside making furniture?" "Yes." he did not hesitate, "Classical Chinese." he said, he started reciting a few poems from old dynasties. Wow! we were definitely miles apart, his classical Chinese, mine English, but we love to talk to each other. I like to be with people with brains and muscles, mind and body, plus a good heart, that would be divine.

One day after lunch, Lin asked if I wanted to see a movie together that evening: there was a new movie just coming out. With aunt Baibai with us, I did not hesitate, I said: "Sure. Longlong would be just fine with aunt Baibai," I said.

The movie theater was not too far, it was company's. Father's company was a big one, they had schools, hospitals, of course theaters too. Lin pulled out his bicycle, I jump up and straddled on the rack at the back of his bicycle. He could not stop laughing, he said women always sat sideways on the rack, only boys straddle, I told him that I straddled the bicycle when I was in labor all the way to the hospital. He laughed so much, he almost fell off the bicycle!

Lin led me to the last row of the seats. The theater was quite full, the movie started soon. Half way during the movie, I felt Lin's hand touching my thigh, his hand did not wander, but I felt his gentle touch. I pretended that I did not notice, I did not move my body at all. After the movie, we rode back to my father's place. I never mentioned his hand on my thigh to him, he did not say anything to me either. But there was an awareness between us that beside the discuss of English, classical Chinese poem, we were man and woman who with feelings toward each other, though Lin was 3 years younger than me.

My maternity leave ended, I decided to take *Longlong* with me back to the paper mill in Inner Mongolia, despite Jin's family's protested. They were far away, they were powerless now, "It is for *Longlong*'s best interest if I could breastfeed him as long as possible." that was my weapon again Jin's family. I was not going back to Beijing!

I took the train to Baoto instead of Beijing with the baby. I left my father, my sister, Jiajia, aunt Baibai and Lin. The brief living in luxury at my father's place revived me. Though the future of bring up a baby by myself in the harsh condition in the paper mill daunted me, I pressed on. The material hardship was far easier to take than the psychological hardship I received from Jin's family.

Chapter 16

Almost Free

I arrived at the paper mill with *Longlong*. *Arxiao* and other friends volunteered to look after *Longlong* when I was teaching. *Longlong* learned to walk at the camp, the joy and laughter he gave us all while watching him wobbled into my arms was a heavenly blessing.

One night, he started high fever, I was so scared, I crushed antibiotic pills, and mixed with sugared water, I made him to take it, it all came back out. Holding him on my laps, seeing his flushed face from fever, I cried helplessly. Two days later, *Longlong*'s fever subsided, he was on his feet again.

Longlong spent his first year through earthquake, then the harsh winter in Inner Mongolia with me. Though he would never remember this, I always wonder what impression left on his psyche make up.

With hectic teaching and taking care of *Longlong*, time went fast, the summer break came. I took the train with *Longlong* heading Beijing again. Jin's family was glad to see their only heir *Longlong* back to them. *Jin Zheng*'s mother said this time, *Longlong* would stay with them when I return to Inner Mongolia. Longlong was old enough to be waned. They would not let *Longlong* live in the harsh condition with me there.

One day when I took *Longlong* with me to visit my mother, while walking on the street with *Longlong*, I happened to see Jin Zheng's best friend Liu, who was at our wedding. Liu married to a lady, and was living with his wife's family, her family lived next to my mother's apartment building.

While talking to Liu on the street, I asked Liu:" Liu, when you have time, could you come and see Jin Zheng again, will you talk to him?"

"What is the matter?" Liu wanted to know more, I told him that Jin Zheng sometimes mention the word "divorce" to me, we already had a son, I hoped that Liu could talk some sense out of Jin Zheng, so that he would not mention the word "divorce" again.

That evening, I was back at Jin's family, since I married to Jin Zheng, I had not been allowed to stay with my mother any more. I became Jin's family possession. At the dining table, I casually mentioned that I happened to see his best friend

Liu at afternoon, before I could finish my sentence. Jin Zheng put down his chip sticks, his face turned to stone, his eyes pieced into mine, and he said: "Liu is MY friend! You have not right to talk to him. Promise me that you will NEVER talk to him!"

I replied: " No problem, if this is your wish. I will not talk to him again." I said it in a composed tone, though inside me I was disgusted with *Jin Zheng*'s cruelty.

Two days later, it was around 5 o'clock in the afternoon, I was busy preparing dinner in the little kitchen, *Longlong* was with me, he followed me in and out of kitchen. It must be a weekend, because *Jin Su* happened to be at home too from her college study.

Then I saw Liu walked down the stone steps from the little gate connecting our courtyard to the outer courtyard. Liu saw me standing at outside of the kitchen shed, he said, "Hi, ...", before he could continue, I cut his greeting short: "Liu, I am not supposed to talk to you..." I said.

Before I could finish my sentence, I saw *Jin Zheng* tailed in behind him. *Jin Zheng* was carried his bicycle on his shoulder, stepping down the steps from the small gate, walked toward the end of the court yard, then he saw Liu standing in front of me.

Jin Zheng threw down the bicycle on the ground, he charged forward, he pushed *Liu* aside, his powerful fist landed in my left eye.

Jin Zheng shouted: "You broke your promise! I will kill you today!" With this he rushed into the kitchen shed, came out with Chinese chopper knife in his hand, *Liu* stepped in between me and *Jin Zheng*, the two men started wrestling for the knife.

Longlong was caught up in this, his eyes opened wide, he started crying hysterically, I pulled him close to me, shield him with my arms, and hands over his eyes, I did not want him to see this ugly side of life.

I moved *Longlong* inside Jin's mother's room, by then his mother walked in from work. *Jin Zheng*'s mother and *Liu* finally talked *Jin Zheng* to give up the knife in his hand. Liu left after a brief talk to *Jin Zheng*. There was no dinner that evening. *Jin Zheng* stayed in his room. I was with *Longlong* in *Jin Zheng*'s mother's room.

Longlong finally fell asleep from exhausting crying. I sat by the bed side, I started stitching soles for *Longlong*'s shoes. *Jin Zheng*'s mother taught me how to make shoes from scrap fabrics. With my left eye swollen almost shut now, I had to tilt my head to use right eye to guide the threaded needle to through each tiny punched hole by a pick.

It was getting really late, *Jin Zheng*'s mother said to me: "*Shaonian*, it's late, you should go back to *Jin Zheng*'s room." I replied: "I cannot go back to his room after what just happened." His mother said: "Look, this room is small, it has just enough room for me, *Jin Shu* and the baby. You cannot stay the night here. Go back to his room!"

I stepped out of her room, the door locked behind me, I stood outside in the courtyard for a few minutes. I wish I could jump onto a bus, and travel back to my mother's place. But I knew I should not, with one eye swollen, black and blue, my mother would be sad if she saw me in this state. I reluctantly walked toward *Jin Zheng*'s room.

The light was still on in his room, I pushed open the door, he was in bed, he looked up at me, and said: "Well, you're coming back after all. Take off your clothes before you can step inside."

I took off my clothes, step into the room, standing naked by the door, *Jin Zheng* ordered me to get into the bed. I lied down in the bed motionless, *Jin Zheng* laid his heavy body on me, and penetrated inside me.

"Now I know what a prostitute feels," I thought to myself, "Lying there to perform your duty with no feelings at all."

That night while lying naked in bed with *Jin Zheng*, who fell to asleep soon after he satisfied himself, I made a vow: "I want to get even for what *Jin Zheng* did to me today."

"I'm physically small, I could not fight him physically but I could get even my way." I reasoned, "I will sleep with a man! And I will not tell him until at his death bed!"

I will tell him: "Listen, *Jin Zheng*, I don't love you, I never loved you though we're married for all these years. I slept with another man!" Upon hearing this, Jin Zheng was so humiliated, he screamed, then he draws his last breath, and he drop dead...

The vision of my revenge was so vivid, I no longer felt a victim, I felt a warrior, I was ready to fight back. I finally fell asleep.

A few days later, while visiting my mother, she asked about the bruise mark on my eye, I pretended that nothing happened. "Oh", I said, "I bumped my face into the door frame."

Two weeks vacation in Beijing went fast, I could not wait for it to end. I told Jin's family that I would detour on the way back to Inner Mongolia, I needed to visit my father, then I would return to the Paper Mill from Taiyuan. I had my revenge plan in mind: I would sleep with carpenter *Xiao Lin*.

This time, Jin's family insisted that *Longlong* would stay with them in Beijing. They would arrange him to go to a nursery nearby. I left Beijing alone, it is OK, I wanted to go to Taiyuan alone to fulfill my plan.

I arrived at Taiyuan, my father was happy to see me as always. I was relieved when I saw Carpenter *Xiao Lin* at my father's apartment. Did he worked at my father's apartment all these past months since I was in Taiyuan the previous summer? I never found out, the fate had it in place: I planed to revenge, *Xiao Lin* was there at my father's apartment as I envisioned.

Xiao Lin was obviously pleased to see me too, we talked while he labored over the wooden pieces like the summer before, the warm bond, the mutual respect was instant like no time lapsed between those months.

The night fell, the rooms at the ladies side were quiet. I did not sleep, I lied in the bed,my mind was busy, "This is it! If I want to get even, this is the night, *Xiao Lin* is at the room across the corridor."

I quietly got out of the bed, started walking along the corridor leading to the other part of the big apartment. I only had my underpants and bra on me, I tip toed along the corridor, upon half way I paused, "Shao-nian, what are you doing?" a thought questioned inside my mind. But the other thought reasoned: "You made a vow, you will revenge. This is the opportunity."

I resumed the tiptoe walking, quietly I reached the foyer connecting to my father's room and the room where Xiao Lin was sleeping. The sound of snoring coming through my father's room, he was sleeping in the sun room at the far end, but his thundering snoring always remind people that he was the master of the house.

I slowly turned the knob of the door of *Xiao Lin*'s room, I pushed it and the door opened! The world seemed stood still. The street light shone through the big window, I could see *Xiao Lin* in bed asleep. I tiptoed over to his bed, gently laid my hand on his shoulder, he woke up right away. He was startled when he saw me standing there by his bed, in the bra and underpants, I did not give him time to think or talk, I laid down beside him.

Xiao Lin moved away a little to make room for me, and he raised up his shoulders, looked into my eyes, he said in a low voice: "I cannot do this to you, this is your father's house!" There was not time to explain or argue, I commanded him in a firm low voice: "Just do it, please!"

Xiao Lin did not utter any more words, he gently pulled me under him. It was not a passionate love-making, but a caring caress and gentle penetrating. *Xiao Lin* did not ejaculate. When it was over, I got up, *Xiao Lin* whispered in my ear: "Don't put your underpants back, just walk back this way, I want to remember you this way forever..."

I woke up late the next morning, my father was already away at his office. After quick breakfast, I walked to *Xiao Lin*'s 'workshop', he was already busy over the wood plank. When he heard me coming in, he raised his head, I could see the grin all over his face, he asked right away: "Hay, did you enjoy it last night, did you have *gaochao*?"

"What is *gaochao*?" I asked, I was completely puzzled by this term. He seemed puzzled too, "What? You don't know *gaochao*? And you are a married woman!"

Xiao Lin went on to explain that the term *gaochao* meant orgasm: When a man and woman have sex together, each would reach the climax of the enjoyment. "Your husband never taught you this?" he asked, I shook my head, "This is the first time I heard this term." *Xiao Lin* then offered to teach me the experience of *gaochao*, I gladly accepted.

That night, after I heard my father's snoring soaring through the corridor, I walked over to *Xiao Lin*'s room. *Xiao Lin* was awake and waiting for me. We played in bed, exploring the points of my body, but I did not experience any differences. For me, a wife's role is to lie down in bed, let man penetrate her, and ejaculate and it is over. Finally *Xiao Lin* had to give up of teaching me gaochao.

On the third day, I was leaving Taiyuan and heading back to Inner Mongolia. *Xiao Lin* joked that I was a slow learner, that he had to teach me next time when I was in town.

I arrived back at the paper mill, the experience with *Xiao Lin* seemed healed me from the wound done by *Jin Zheng*. *Xiao Lin* became a refuge for me to escape from the reality of my marriage to *Jin Zheng*. I started writing to *Xiao Lin*, he was married, I was married, we as a mature adults could talk about life in a mature way.

I felt the tender love toward *Xiao Lin*, it was the first experience of this tender love, not because we had sexual connection. It was different from the sexual experience with *Wang Junxiang*. *Xiao Lin* and I would talk and laugh and talk. With *Wang Junxiang*, he would sit there silently, and watching me move around in the room contently. At that time, *Wang Junxiang* finally had a girlfriend. We would say hi when we occasionally bumped into each other in the paper mill. *Xiao Lin*, though hundreds of miles away in Taiyuan, through letters and just thoughts, I felt I was in love with Xiao Lin intellectually, not sexually. I did not care if I would ever learn about *gaochou*. I felt the thought of *Xiao Lin* was a *gaochou* for me. It made me smile inside. That sweet feeling I seldom experienced ever since I grew up.

The regular movie projection team arrived at the paper mill, that night they were showing a Romania movie. It was about a famous violinist, his tragic love story and his violin performance. I thought of the tender love I had toward Xiao Lin, the tears welled up in my eyes, since it was in the dark, no one could see me, I let it run down my face freely. His violin music etched in my mind.

(About 15 years later in US, late one night, I was working in the kitchen in my restaurant, I was all by myself, a violin music came on from my radio, I froze in my motion. It was the same violin tune I was crying with in the dark in Inner Mongolia! I pushed down the button of recording. Finally I had that violin music on a cassette. A few years later, one of my Taichi student Stefan happened to be a violin teacher, and he was from Romania. I mentioned my first experience with that movie and the violinist and his haunting music. A week later, Stefan came to my work place, he asked me to sit down by a table. He took out his violin from the box, there Stefan performed the whole violin piece for me!)

One day after my teaching, I walked toward my room, there I saw *Jin Zheng* standing in front of the room, I could not believe my eyes. There Jin Zheng suddenly appeared in the paper mill, like he was dropped from sky!

"Jin Zheng," I greeted him, "How come you are here?"

"I just want to visit you, and see how the life is in Inner Mongolia." he said casually. I led him into the room, cooked lunch for him. Later on in the afternoon, while I was teaching, he said he would walk around the camp himself. Soon the news of *Jin Zheng*'s arrival was known all over the factory. *Jin Zheng* was obvious aware of his tall, strong physical feature, and handsome face, he walked around the camp always with his chin up.

The evening came, I prepared the bed, so that we two could sleep in the same bed. *Jin Zheng* fell asleep soon, I reasoned that he must be tired from long hours train ride, plus walked around the camp. I lied beside him quietly, I was glad that he did not demand sex, that I could rest too. I drifted into my sleep.

Suddenly I was woken by a push on my shoulder. I opened my eyes, I saw *Jin Zheng* standing beside the bed, hovering over me. "Wake up, wake up." he said. I sat up in bed.

Jin Zheng started talking: "I came to Inner Mongolia with olive branch in one hand, and knife in another hand."

I was still half asleep, I wondered silently: "What is this poetic 'olive branch' to do in the middle of night?"

Jin Zheng continued, "I knew there is no love between us, though we're married. I suspect that you have a lover in Inner Mongolia, that is why I am here. Today I walked around the camp and talked with many people here, they all praised you, they said that you don't have a lover. So I decide to let the fate decide our lives."

I sat in the bed motionless and emotionless, I did not understand the situation fully yet. *Jin Zheng* then pulled out the hand behind him, his was holding the big kitchen knife! I woke up fully, this time there was no one there, the whole world seemed stopped, only the ultimate quietness of the open desert in the middle of the night.

Upon seeing *Jin Zheng*'s knife, I was still motionless, and emotionless. (Now looking back, it might be the survival instinct, had I started screaming, fighting, he might have used the knife.) *Jin Zheng* continue his "poetic" speech when seeing me sat there motionless.

"There were two bowels on the kitchen table, one bowl is filled with plain water, the other bowel is water with cyanide. Now, get up, go to the table and drink from one of the bowels. If you dare to scream, I will kill you right here!"

My mind finally started racing, it was futile to fight with a strong man with a knife hovering over me. I blamed myself for this: "God, is this the penalty I receive because I slept with other men? So be it."

I took the watch, my father's gift for my wedding, off my wrist, I laid it down beside the pillow, and looked up into *Jin Zheng*'s eyes, "This is for *Longlong*."

After saying that, I calmly get off the bed, walked passed *Jin Zheng*, straight to the table in the kitchen table. I picked up a bowel with no hesitation, and drank it all in one gulp. Then I put down the bowel. Nothing happened to me.

Jin Zheng said: "The fate is on your side this time. Now it is my turn to drink another bowel." he picked up the other bowel.

"Please don't..." I reached over to the bowel, he pushed me aside, held up to bowel to his mouth and started drinking, water dripped down his chin, down to his chest, and down his body, dripped down to the floor. *Jin Zheng* emptied the bowel, and put down the bowel on the table. He stepped out of the kitchen, then he fell down to the floor, he started shivering, grinding his teeth, his body curled up.

I rushed to him. I knelt down on the floor beside him, held him in my arms. After all *Jin Zheng* was dying because of me, I felt sorry for his death, I started crying, my tears run down my face, they fell on *Jin Zheng*'s face, suddenly, his eyes opened, he stopped shivering, his body relaxed up, he started laughing loudly.

"it looks like that you still care about me. I was faking all this, I wanted to test you, maybe after all, our marriage can be saved." *Jin Zheng* said while lying on the floor looking up at my tear soaked face.

I felt like a brick just hit on my head. I felt sick, I was speechless. *Jin Zheng* jumped up to his feet, he jumped back to the bed and he fell back to sleep soon. Lying in bed beside him, in the middle of the night in the middle of the desert in Inner Mongolia, I cried silently this time it was for myself.

Jin Zheng said he came with one hand with olive branch, and one hand with knife. Tonight through his knife, he offered his olive branch: our marriage could be saved. I did not want either his knife or his olive branch.

The next morning, *Jin Zheng* appeared in good mood, he said that he would stay for a couple of more days, then he would head back to Beijing. A day passed without any drama, *Jin Zheng* mingled with people well while I was in the classes.

The third day, I went to the post office which is just outside the factory building, it was far from where the school was. I walked out of the post office, and started looking through a couple of mails, I was expecting *Xiao Lin*'s letter since I wrote to him. There it was! A letter from Taiyuan, but not my father's handwriting. I eagerly opened it, before I could read the letter, a hand from behind reached over my shoulder, and grabbed the letter. I looked back, it was *Jin Zheng*!

"What is this letter, let me have a look." he started reading Xiao Lin's letter, his face changed as he read more, I could see that he was furious, but he controlled his temper since we were out in the public with people around, he said to me in a low voice: "Come with me! I want to talk to you." *Jin Zheng* started walking toward the far end of the open warehouse, where pyramids of baled reeds stored.

We passed the pyramids, we walked outside the factory boundary, toward the reservoir. *Jin Zheng* stopped between the small sand dunes. With nobody around, and nobody could see us, *Jin Zheng* slapped on my face, "You slut!" He then started beating on my body with his fists and feet, I was rolling on the sand, curled up to fend off his blow. What a contrast of rolling on the same sand dunes. Before I was a carefree tomboy, trying to ride those horses, falling and rolling around in the sand with laughters. But this time with the same sand dunes, I was beaten by *Jin Zheng*. After a while, he was tired of beating and venting. He left me on the sand, and he started walking back. "I will see you tonight again." he told me.

I never had a chance to read Xiao Lin's letter, it was confiscated by *Jin Zheng*. *Jin Zheng* was clever enough that no sign of beaten could be seen on my face. I taught the classes as usual that afternoon. I blocked my mind out not to think of the night. After what I went through with him the previous night, I did not care. I stared at the death's face once already.

When I finished classes, I returned to my room, *Jin Zheng* was waiting for me. He said that he was going to report *Xiao Lin* to his work unit, to expose his adultery, Xiao Lin could lose his job. I begged him not to do that, not to hurt *Xiao Lin* publicly. I offered to write a letter to *Xiao Lin*'s wife, confessing it was me that caused his fall. Jin Zheng demanded that I needed to write a letter to my father about my sleeping with Xiao Lin. Otherwise, he would write to the company publicly. I thought that by writing to my father myself, by writing to Xiao Lin's wife, at least it was settled privately. Hopefully *Xiao Lin*'s wife would forgive him and his marriage would be saved.

Jin Zheng took my offer, he made me to write those letters right in front of him, then he wrote a letter to my father too. I never had an chance to see Xiao Lin again. I heard later that my father banished him from his apartments, and he was sent to work at a far away construction site, but his marriage was saved. My father never talked to me about my sleeping with *Xiao Lin*. I knew I disappointed him deeply. Even that I never told him how *Jin Zheng* and his family treated me, I did not want him to feel sad. It was my own decision, and I could shoulder all this.

The night came, after the door was closed. Jin Zheng ordered me to strip off my clothes. I stood naked on the floor, he demanded me to tell him the details of my encounter with *Xiao Lin*. I offered nothing. I admitted that I slept with him. That was all. Jin Zheng went into rage again, he pushed me on the floor, and got on top of me, "Tell me what you did together?" he demanded. I was silent. He got up, light up his cigarette, with a deep draw, he got down with his knee on my body, he pushed the burning cigarette on my chest between my breasts.

"This is your scarlet letter! You will carry your adultery mark for the rest of your life." *Jin Zheng* fumed. Scarlet letter? Suddenly, I remembered that was one of his favorite novels. He even handed it over to me to read once.

I did not like the main character. *Jin Zheng* adored the stories like *The Count of Monte Cristo*, *Scarlet Letter*, or *Les Miserables*. I did not like the theme of relentless revenge or pursuing. My heroes were generous, benevolent, my heroes were self-sacrifice to save. Not the characters who persecute those already down and under.

The intense pain from the burning cigarette brought my flash memory back to the reality. *Jin Zheng* threw the squashed cigarette on the floor, he then straddled upon me, he unzipped his pants, he started thrusting his penis into me. I closed my eyes, I kept my lips closed too, so that I would not cry. While *Jin Zheng* violently thrusting into me, my mind was racing.

"When all this ends, I will to go to a doctor, I will ask him to take out my woman's organ, it caused me so much troubles because of it," I thought. Tears started streaming down my face, was it because of the pain from cigarette burning, or the pain from *Jin Zheng*'s thrusting, or the pain from my heart?

Jin Zheng went into orgasm, he pulled out his penis, with one hand holding it, he hovered over my face, he started smearing his semen on my face, then down over my breasts, he mumbled with rage, but I did not hear any of his words any more, I shut my ears. I kept my eyes shut tighter, my lips tighter, so that the mixture of my tears and his semen would not enter me, would not hurt me. All I could say in my mind was: "When all this ends, I'll ask a doctor to take my woman's part out.... When all this ends, I'll ask a doctor to take my woman's part out." It was my saving mantra.

The memory of the rest of the night was blank. All I could remember was the next morning, *Jin Zheng* left the camp, before he stepped out of the door, he said, "I am divorcing you! When you come back to Beijing, don't come back to me."

Chapter 17

Final Divorce

Jin Zheng left the Paper Mill, life resumed to the normal routine, I taught at the school, nobody seemed to know anything happened between me and *Jin Zhang*. I did not tell *Arxiao*, I did not tell my family about *Jin Zheng*'s coming to Inner Mongolia. What happened seemed too much for me to describe it by words to anyone. I did not want to relive any second of it. I pushed all this in the remote corner of my psyche, so that I could live a normal life.

Of course I never heard from carpenter *Xiao Lin* after I wrote those letters to Taiyuan, one to me father and one to his wife. *Xiao Lin* probably forever resented me for suddenly writing to his wife, only in my heart, I did my best trying to save him from *Jin Zheng*'s relentless revenge of having him exposed publicly, losing his job, and marriage.

It was 1978, almost 10 years since I arrived Inner Mongolia, quite a few people managed to leave the paper mill and returned to their home cities. Most of the girls from my group had left paper mill under various medical conditions, I finally found out that though you might be healthy, you could still get a doctor to write you a fake diagnosis with fake x-ray photos. Then by giving cartons of cigarettes, you could be released from the camp and be allowed to return to your home city legally.

Though hesitant and doubtful, I took my friends advice, especially I was married with family in Beijing. I went through the same methods. The doctor was building his new house, I went there, volunteered my labor of mixing cement and mud, of shoveling the mixture to the rooftop. During the shoveling, it reminded me the transportation squad, we did so much shoveling, it reminded me of shoveling mud to the rooftop of the little kitchen at Jin Zheng's court yard the day before I gave birth.

At the end I got doctor's diagnosis and through him, I got a fake x-ray photo. My next step was to save money to buy cartons of cigarettes. When those cartons were delivered to those in charge. I was officially released from the paper mill.

Arxiao and other friends organized a farewell dinner. I was eager to move back to Beijing, though I was also comprehensive of returning to Beijing to face Jin Zheng, the divorce, my son... but I did not tell anyone at the camp. No need to burden others with my problems.

That last night, after everyone left, I finally sat down to let the reality sink into me: "I am leaving Inner Mongolia after 10 years for good!"

Packing was easy. I did not want any thing to take back as souvenir. Only a few of my clothes. It was getting late, there was a gentle knock at the door. I opened the door, there was *Wang Junxiang* standing at the door with his usual shy smile. I said:"I thought you would be at the dinner party." He said he was busy at work. I let him in, he sat down in a chair.

I continued my packing while talking to *Wang Junxiang*. How was he and his girlfriend? *Wang Juxiang* said fine, they were planning the marriage. As usual, *Wang Junxiang* was content sitting and watching me doing my own chores. Finally when I told *Wang Junxiang*, it was late, he looked into my eyes, and said: "Just one more time. Tomorrow you will be gone, I may never see you again."

I did not have the heart to refuse him. I turned off the light, and led him to the bed, we took our clothes off, and lied down, *Wang Junxiang* held me close to him, he started sobbing, I tried to comfort him. *Wang Junxiang* was so distraught for my leaving, that he could not bright himself to erection. We two laid there together, finally *Wang Junxiang* gave up of having erection. When he left the room, he said that he would not be there to say goodbye to me the next day.

I did not have any memory of the next day. It was uneventful. Arriving at railway station in Beijing, I went straight to my mother's apartment! A relief of not going to *Jin Zheng*'s place. My mother already received verbal notice from *Jin Zheng* of her adulterous daughter who would be ostracized from Jin's family. Mother was all smile when she saw me back to live with her. All she mentioned to me was: "People in Jin's family are not good-hearted."

But I went back to Jin's family the next day after I arrived back in Beijing. I wanted to see my son *Longlong*. *Jin Zheng* was waiting for me. He filed divorce paper, he needed me to go with him to the registration office to finalize it. I went with him to the office, since both parties consented with divorce, the procedure was easy. *Jin Zhang* played the role of a victim, he said it was all my fault, he needed to be compensated. There was no dispute, I left all furniture my father had them made by *Xiao Lin* to *Longlong*, I left all the money I saved to them. I left *Jin Zheng*'s family with only my clothes on my back.

Even that was not enough for *Jin Zheng*, at the registration office, he insisted that on the divorce document, adultery was the reason for divorce and had to be written on the decree, so that I could not find a good job, I would carry the bad reputation for the rest of my life. To help the divorce paper finalize fast, I did not say much at the office, the document was granted, written in the way as *Jin Zheng* demanded.

Our divorce was final soon after I returned to Beijing. I asked the family to allow me to see *Longlong* on the weekends, and that *Longlong* could stay with me at my mother's place overnight. Jin's family agreed. At the meantime, I got a temporary job as English teacher at Beijing No.156 High School. It was my former No.6 Girls High School. I did not see all my former teachers, no Zhou Laoshi, my former English teacher there. I was assigned to teach grade 1 for the junior high school.

I was pleased that I had a job as soon as I returned to Beijing though it was a temporary one. I was determined to be good at my new school. Very soon, the head of the English Department announced that I would be teaching grade 3 in senior high. That was an honor, most of the students in senior high were taller than me. I spent more of my time at the school, with students, with my work. But I would look forward to the weekends, I would hurry to *Jin Zheng*'s place after the school. I could take *Longlong* with me, he could spend the night me at my mother's place.

We would go to parks, I started teaching *Longlong* simple English too. At night seeing him lying beside me, I was happy. "As long as I could see *Longlong* on weekends, it would be worth it." that's what I told myself , because there was a price to pay to see him on weekends.

Though by then we were legally divorced, *Jin Zheng* told me, it was my fault, that he needed to be compensated: if ever he wanted sex, he would call me, I would go to his place in the early mornings, to satisfy his sexual demand. The reward was the weekend time with *Longlong*. Thus was his arrangement.

I was always reluctant to answer the phone call in the office. At that time, there was no private phone service in individual household. Only public phone service. When people in the office called out: "Wu Shao-nian, phone call for you." It would be *Jin Zheng*'s. Then next morning, I had to get on the first bus to ride to the other side of the city. Sitting in the seat on the empty bus, I wondered how life evolved: "when I was a student at high school, I always rode the first bus to go to school. Now I am riding the first bus to go to have sex, so that I could see my son."

It was still very early in *Jin Zheng*'s courtyard, I slowly push open their heavy gate, so that the gate would not give noise to wake up the people in the courtyard. Walked lightly to pass *Jin Zheng*'s mother's room, I slowly pushed open the door of *Jin Zheng*'s room. He would be waiting for me.

When *Jin Zheng* got on top of me, having sex, he tried to put his face next to mine, I turned my face away, he got annoyed, he slapped my face, saying: "You are having sex with me, but you still don't like me?"

"Like?" I rebuked his selection of the word inside my mind, "I **despise** you. I am having sex, because I want to be with my son." When he finished his sex demand, I put on my clothes, and walked quietly away, I needed to hurry to my school.

Back in the office in the school, a teacher asked:" Hi, Wu Shao-nian, how come that your face looked red, is it swollen?" I pretended that nothing happened, I said:"Maybe I put on some weight, so my face looked swollen." That was a feeble excuse, I was glad that no one else probed more.

One day I was at home, suddenly I heard *Jin Zheng*'s voice outside, "*Wu Shao-nian, Wu Shao-nian*, come out!" I went out, there was *Jin Zheng* standing by the curb of the street, hands on his bicycle handles. I walked toward him, he demanded: "Tell me, who else did you sleep with beside *Xiao Lin*?" I said: "None else." *Jin Zheng* asked again, I said no again. Then *Jin Zheng* said: "This is my third time to ask you who else...?" I said none again. Upon that, Jin Zheng pulled out a letter from an upper pocket of his shirt and threw it to my face, "Read it!" he demanded.

It was a letter from *Wang Junxiang* to Jin Zheng, *Wang* admitted having sex with me. That was life, I thought I could save him, but he turned himself in. Later I heard that after I returned to Beijing, *Jin Zheng* wrote letters to people in paper mill, telling them that I was adulterous with a carpenter in Taiyuan, *Wang Junxiang* out of fear, wrote a letter to *Jin Zheng.*

Because I was standing out in the street, *Jin Zheng*, though very angry, could not beat me in the public, he pulled the letter out of my hands and said: "I will make *Wang Junxiang* pay for this." he rode off on his bicycle.

About a month later, while I was busy at the office, I was told that there was a man from Inner Mongolia who wanted to see me. I met him at the gate of the school. He introduced me that he was from the court of Inner Mongolia. They received a letter from *Jin Zheng* filing a case on *Wang Junxiang*, accusing him raping me. The Inner Mongolia court sent this investigator to talk to me about the case.

I took the investigator to a small quiet restaurant near the school. Sitting by the table in a quiet corner, I told the investigator about my life in Inner Mongolia, the transportation squad, the love of *Wang Junxiang* had toward me, my marriage to Jin Zheng... that was the first time I told anyone about my marriage. By the end, I told the investigator: "Wang Junxiang did not rape me. He loved me, and I returned his love by sleeping with him, because I **wanted** to do it. If you need to put someone in jail for this case, put me in!"

Before the investigator left me, he said that he doubted there's any evidence against *Wang Junxiang* about rape case. He added: surely if I want, I could file a case against *Jin Zheng* of raping me! He handed over me his card: "If you ever come to Inner Mongolia again, please stop by." he said.

Weeks passed, I continued seeing *Jin Zheng* on his sex demand as long as I could have *Longlong* with me on weekends. *Jin Zheng* mentioned one day that whatever I said to the investigator, the Inner Mongolia did not proceed with his rape case against *Wang Junxiang*.

I never heard about *Wang Junxiang* again. Because of *Jin Zheng*'s letters to people in the Paper Mill of my adultery with *Xiao Lin*. I felt I brought shame to myself, to Arxiao, to friends who always looked up to me. I was their role model. I did not have the time, energy to go back to explain to everyone of my marriage. I decided to cut the cord, let *Jin Zheng* write whatever he wanted to anyone in the paper mill. I needed to move on. I cut off my connection with Inner Mongolia, I did not want to see or hear any news from Paper Mill.

Life without Jin's family was carefree. One day I had a pair of turquoise blue corduroy trousers with bell bottom on. The bell-bottom trousers became a fad, students love it when I wore it in the class. It was Friday, in the afternoon after the class, I rode the bus to Jin's family, it was the day I could take *Longlong* with me back to my mother's place.

Jin Zheng walked in to his mother's room, when he saw me, he said he needed to talk to me in his room. When I entered his room, *Jin Zheng* sat at the edge of the bed, "Take off your trousers," he demanded, "A woman like you does not deserve to wear this fashion thing."

When I took off the trousers, he picked it up, then with a pair of scissors, he started cutting the trousers with venom. When finished, he threw the shredded trousers down on the floor. He started his usual psychological belittling: "A dirty woman like you only deserve to lay in the ditch by the roadside …"

I had my way to ward off his psycho bullets, I turned it into a game. Whenever he opened his venomous mouth, I started translating his words into English, by this, I did not waste my time with him, I was just practicing my English skill.

Jin Zheng continued, "I will always hunt you down, beat you down. Even one day when I build a skyscraper of my life, and you live in a small hut by the road, I will still tear your hut down!" "What a strange poem, skyscraper, and little hut," I wondered in my mind, and lost in my thought, I blurred out my translation audibly. "What are you talking?" Jin Zheng demand. It brought me back to his room. His "poem" disgusted me, at that moment, I made a vow, I would go to places far far away, that *Jin Zheng* could never touch my little hut.

By then *Jin Zheng*'s mother walked into the room, upon seeing me standing in the middle of the room with only underpants on, she asked why. *Jin Zheng* told her that I did not deserve to wear a nice fashionable clothes. Jin's mother said: "Son, you two are already divorced. You can not fight like this. Shao-nian has the right too, she probably can sue you for this."

Hearing her words, *Jin Zheng* said: "OK, from today on, you don't have to come to me for sex anymore, we don't need to see each other any more. But under one condition: You cannot take *Longlong* with you on weekends anymore!"

After that *Jin Zheng* asked me to leave, I was only in my underpants, *Jin Zheng* said a dirty woman like me could walk in the street like this. Jin's mother stepped in, she offered me to wear her oversized trousers.

That evening, I walked back to my mother's place, my mother looked up and asked: "Where is *Longlong*?" I told her of *Jin Zheng*'s words, my mother replied:"We will miss

Longlong, but I am glad that you two are not seeing each other anymore. The Jin's family is a cold-hearted family." Then she asked where was the beautiful corduroy trousers I wore that morning, I told her that one of the students liked it so much, I gave it to her.

Months passed, I kept my promise not to see *Longlong*. But how could anyone stopped a mother from seeing her son? One late morning, I rode the bus toward Jin's family, I knew that was the time when everyone was at work, I wanted to see *Longlong* at his kindergarten. The kindergarten was near their place on the main street. Late morning was a good time, probably few parents would be there.

I walked through the gate, nobody was there, I then enter the inner courtyard, I knew *Longlong*'s class was in the room on the north side of the yard. Nobody could be seen in the yard. Stepping up the stone steps, I looked in through the glass on the door, there they were, about 20 children all sitting in small chairs in the center of the room, they were sitting facing the door.

I looked again, their faces all looked similar, tender, smiling, it took me a few seconds to spot *Longlong*, he was sitting right in the center of the row. I recognized him, because he was the only child not laughing or smiling. Our eyes met, I saw tears running down his face.

I slowly pushed the door open, and I stepped inside the room, nobody around, except children sitting in the chairs, laughing, smiling. I started walking toward *Longlong*, I stretched out my arms, suddenly the world seemed faded away, the children's sounds faded away, everything seemed in slow motion: I arms were stretched out, I wanted to embrace him, I wanted to wipe his tear washed face.... but I froze half way; *Longlong* lowered his tear soaked face, he raised up one hand to stop me from holding him!

I froze there for a few seconds, I was so close to him, I could almost pull him into my arms and embrace him. But I backed out before he raised up his head.

The following days had been tough for me. I could not forget his tear washed face, his little hand raised to stop me. I made a decision: it is better to let him forget me and live a normal life. If it was so hard for me, an adult, it would be ten times harder for his tender heart to bear all this. Let him forget me, so he can grow up as a normal man. No, I don't want any more tears for him!

Longlong was the last thread that connected me and *Jin Zheng*, though it was painful, but I finally cut it off. Years passed, I moved far far away from *Jin Zheng*, from England, from America, through my sister Shao-hua, I requested many times, *Jin Zheng*'s family always refused me meeting *Longlong*.

But I often meet *Longlong* in my dreams, he was always a small boy as I was with him.

That was my first marriage with *Jin Zheng*, though physically together was less than 2 months, the psychological effect lasted life time.

Chapter 18

Steel Plant

I did not have to ride a bus across the city early in the morning to answer *Jin Zheng*'s demand for sex any more, I could not go to see *Longlong* on weekends either, my life changed significantly. I now had time for myself. The freedom I had after the tie with Jin's family cut was tempting and could be "dangerous". Maybe *Wang Junxiang*'s words in his love letter were right, I was always a wild galloping horse ... I was never a "normal person" following the crowd or society's codes. I follow my own path or march at my own drum beat and seldom calculate the price to pay .

The money I saved through the years I left to *Longlong* after divorce. Money was never a real problem for me, I was always frugal to myself. I could save money easily. Soon I saved enough to buy a bicycle. It was a new style, small wheels, sky blue color! The bicycle gave me more freedom.

With my earlier school days sports efforts, I decided to try Wushu. I saw people doing exercises in the morning near our place. The place was not too far from my mother's apartment. It was a big open space in front of government's *Ministry of Building & Construction*. Several groups of people did Taichi and other forms of exercise there. I went there one morning to observe what people were doing there. I decided to learn from one shifu. He was in his 70's, tall and slim, He only had a couple of students. He was not teaching Taichi, but chaquan, a style of Chinese wushu. Those days, wushu meant martial art in external style, fast, energetic. Taichi was only for older people.

Traditionally, you should not just walk over to a master asking him to teach you, that was considered rude. He would not accept you. You needed his students or someone he knew to recommend you to him. But I did not know anyone who was connected with the master. I decided to go there every morning anyway. I would observe the master teaching his few young students doing stretching, and movements. Then I would practice later by myself somewhere else.

A couple of months passed, I felt confident enough to go there in the morning and started practicing alone. But I chose the spot there close enough that I hoped the master could glance over and seeing me doing HIS style. It worked! The third morning when I just started practice, the master came to me, he said: "I saw you doing *chaquan* here alone, do you want to join the group?" Thus I became *Liu Shifu*'s third student.

I fell in love with wushu's beauty of movements. I practiced it with same zest as my love of going to school, or my love of swimming, or my love of studying English. I got up at 5 o'clock every morning, I would be the first one there at the training spot. Soon I became *Liu Shifu*'s favorite student.

Beside *chaquan*, Liu start teaching me long tassel sword. Long tassel sword became my favorite wushu. I remember the thrill of purchasing my first sword. It was all that I could afford it at the time. The blade was a bit long according to my height, the handle was a bit big to my hands, but it was a nice heavyweight sword. I bought it, I had to have it altered to fit to my hands and height. I still practice with it now, after 30 years. Though the tassel were worn, the sheath worn, it was repaired several times, it was not an expensive sword, I could now easily replace it with other expensive ones. It was my first sword.

At No.156 High we had a new English teacher Linda. Linda was three years older than me, both of her parents died in the Cultural Revolution by Red Guards persecution. She was living with her aunt. She was hired as a temporary English teacher like me, because we were not college graduates, we were *Laosanjie*. Maybe that was the reason we became close friends. We called each other with English names, she chose Linda, mine was *Youngster*, which was the direct translation of my Chinese name *Shao-nian*.

Linda was assigned to teach grade one for junior high students, I was the teacher for grade 3 for senior high students. She adored my English skill. Suddenly I found another sister, we would do things together whenever we had free time outside the school. Linda would spend the night at my mother's place with me. She loved my family, she asked if she could move in with us. Knowing her loss of her parents, my mother had no objection. So Linda became a member of the family. Linda never told us how her parents died from Red Guards persecution, probably it was too painful. We all lived through it, we all heard other's stories, we had full sympathy toward her.

It seemed that though I had three sisters and one brother, most of my grown up time, I was not with them, I always ended with an adopted sister. Linda was tall, though not as tall as *Jin Su*, she was also a strong built. She looked older than her age. When we walked together, occasionally, people thought we were mother and daughter!

Linda was not athletic, I could not get her to practice wushu with me. But she was a great cook, that was excellent, since my mother was not in cooking, I could cook to feed Jin's family, but my interest was not in it. Now we loved the time at dinner table, my mother laughed loud with Linda's humorous stories she cooked up along with her delicious dishes. Life seemed sweet again. I found myself laughing again.

Before one year passed since I worked as a temporary teacher in Beijing No.156 High School, the government issued a new policy, it stated that parents of those *Zhiqing* (youths returned to their cities from the countryside) could retire early to let their children replace their job place, so that those *Zhiqing* could have a regular job in government units. At that time, no individual business was allowed. Everyone belonged to a government work unit.

My mother decided to retire from her position in the clinic in *Beijing Steel Rolling plant*, so that I could have a real regular work. I left No.156 High School. This was a blow to Linda, she worried that she had to move out, but we assured that she was a member of the family, so Linda continued teaching at No. 156 High. We still went out together whenever we had time together after work.

My mother was a pharmacist at the clinic, since I did not have any knowledge nor experience remotely related to pharmacy, the Logistic department which managed the clinic assigned me to work with their cleaning crew.

The work was a big contrast from teaching senior high school students at No. 156. I could not wear corduroy bell bottom pants, or any fashion at work any more, instead I wore denim overall, with denim cap, it reminded me of paper mill again. But it was an official regular job after all.

We worked in shifts as the steel workers work in shifts. Our job was to sweep the streets in the plant, make soda drinks and deliver them to all the workshops. Steel rolling was a heavy industry, the hot iron had to be melted in big furnaces, then poured into molds to roll into different sizes of steel bars for construction.

Most of the workers in the cleaning crew were older workers, only 3 younger workers like me, replacing parent's job. Work was simple, a broomstick to sweep the streets in the plant, or a push cart to deliver the drinks to the workshops in the plant.

During the break, all the cleaning workers would gather in the small room, the room was a bare concrete cell with one big long wooden table and long benches on both sides. Crew members would sit down, have tea. Most of them would pull out the cigarettes, they would puff and chat. The smoke soon filled up the room.

I preferred to sit aside at the far corner of the room. I did not like the smell of cigarette, it reminded me of *Jin Zheng*. I did not care much of their petty chats. I would lift my work cap, pull out a folded piece of paper, I would read my English study.

It was odd at the beginning for all the workers seeing me reading English, they would make some funny remarks. But soon they got used to me reading in a corner, I did not bother anyone, they would leave me alone, though I was definitely an odd ball to all of them.

My wushu practice got better and better as time went on. I found myself attracting crowd when I practiced. With Liu shifu's coaching, my long tassel would fly, dazzle the onlookers eyes. I would toss the sword in the air, and then catch it with my hand at the back!

I noticed there was a loyal onlooker there among them, he was an older man with a pair of rimmed glasses, he looked like in his 70's. One day, he walked over to me, "Miss, I really enjoy watching your doing long tassel sword, can you teach me what you are doing?" he asked. I was shocked. He was an old man, Wushu was too fast for him to learn. "This may be a little bit fast, Why don't you learn Taichi, it is slow, easy for you." I suggested to him.

The old man gave me a shy smile, then he told me that he watched me everyday, he loved my moving with sword, he simply wanted to be a friend to me. If he could know me even if he had to learn my sword, he would give it a try. I was taken by his sincere confession, and his complement to my sword practice. So Mr. Fan became a friend, an old-man friend.

Mr. Fan got his degree in architecture in Germany, he was a senior architect at the *Ministry of Building & Construction* Research Institute. Since he worked and lived close to my mother's place, he came to the training spot in the morning to watch me practice, then after that he would buy me breakfast and we would talk over the table.

Mr. Fan did not learn any Wushu from me, but he learned many of my stories. I poured out my heart to him. At least sharing my stories to him would not hurt him like it would if I've told my own mother and father. There is no way I would tell my parents what I had experienced. I did not want to cause any pain to my parents. But sharing my stories with Mr. Fan helped me to release the pain and heal me from the wound of the marriage and divorce to *Jin Zheng*.

I told Mr. Fan that I hoped one day I could go to lands far away, so that *Jin Zheng* could not touch me or hurt me any more. That was one of the reasons that I never ceased to study English, I wanted to be better equipped if I could ever have an opportunity to go abroad. Mr. Fan wholehearted agreed. Through those breakfast mornings, Mr. Fan also told me stories of his study days in Germany.

Oh, beside the study, there was always good time spent in the bars in the evenings. The German girls loved him, because he would make them happy. They would always go back to look for him. I didn't quite understand it at the time. Mr. Fan did not elaborate it either. Now looking back, Mr. Fan was probably very good at sex, so the German girls were made happy.

One day, Mr. Fan gave me a gift, a small hand-held electric massager. I asked what it was for. "Shao-nian, now I've heard your stories, I want you to enjoy life, to be happy. You told me that you never had *gaochao*, try this massager, and see what will happen."

Though I didn't quite understand the role of massager, I knew it might help me to experience orgasm. That night, I waited for Linda to fall asleep. Linda always slept like a log, she often snored when she was asleep. But that night, I did not mind her snoring. I plugged the massager, her snoring might well cover the faint humming sound of the massager. I started moving the massager gently exploring over my body, then I found the location, my whole body started shaking, I moaned silently... I was stunned by my first experience of orgasm. Later I learned the term masturbation, though it sounded negative, I own Mr. Fan for giving me a chance to experience the ecstasy and pleasure of orgasm.

One day through a book I was studying, I read the article of a sermon, the phrase: "Man proposes and God disposes" struck a chord with me. I thought: "This is exactly what my life is. Though I always thought that I am a strong girl, a good girl, but in life I failed miserably, married once, committed adultery, divorced, lost my son... maybe what was missing in my life is God!"

It was a New Year's Day morning, it was my New Year's resolution. I woke up Linda. "It's holiday today," Linda grumped in bed with her eyes still closed, "why up so early?"

I said: "Linda, today we are going to look for God!" Upon hearing this, Linda's eyes opened, "Where is God?" she asked, now she was awake. I told her to get up and I will show her where God was.

The weather was not good, when we pushed our bicycles out of the apartment building, the wind was strong, the sky looked yellow because of the sand. But we pushed on, with our heads ducked down to avoid the sand blown into our eyes, our whole body leaned forward to peddle the bicycles toward downtown.

I knew there was a church building in west downtown area, because it had high spikes on the rooftop unlike most buildings in Beijing. Even with strong wind, we got there in 30 minutes. When we arrived at the church, the gate was not locked. We put our bicycles by the gate, walked toward the church. The door was not locked either, I pushed open the huge heavy door apart, and stepped inside, Linda followed behind me.

Wow, this was the first time to be in a church. There was not a soul in the building, only dim lights through the long tall narrow windows. We walked forward toward the altar, the sound of our footsteps echoed down from the high ceiling, the atmosphere was intimidating ..

Suddenly a priest appeared from behind the altar. A tall, bonny figure in a long robe. His face was somber, he asked why we were there, I was going to tell him that I was looking for God, but somehow, when the words came out of my mouth, they changed, I ended up asking him if there was another church in the city.

"Are you looking for the Protestant church?" the priest wanted to make sure. I simply nodded my head, though I did not know then what "Protestant" meant, I wanted to leave, I felt cold. "This is a Catholic church. The Protestant church you are look for is at *Chongwenmen*, the east side of downtown." the figure in robe informed me. I pulled Linda's hand, we quickly backed out of the building.

"Linda, let's keep going, maybe we will find God in the other church." Linda shook her head, reluctantly, she followed me to continue our head-ducking, shoulder-forward, peddling eastward.

After asking around a few times near *chongwenmen*, we finally found the Protestant church, it was no different than other buildings around it. There was no spikes on the rooftop. The wooden fence gate was locked. The church was sitting on the corner of the street, so I walked around the wall, and saw a small door on the side. I pushed the button of the door bell on the wall.

A few seconds passed, then the door was pulled ajar, a round face appeared through the gap between the door and the wall. I explained to the face that I was looking for God, if that was the right place.

Suddenly the door was flown open wide, the round face changed to a round figure, middle height, he could be any man walking on the street, he was not in a robe and there was a welcoming smile all over his face.

"Come on in! Girls." Pastor Kan said with his arms open wide while stepping on the side to give way to us. The stone path led right into the kitchen. There Pastor Kan had us seated down, and started making tea while chatting with me. Briefing? I guess.

I eagerly told Pastor Kan that I got married, and divorced, I worked at a steel plant, I practice wushu in the morning, I could not stop telling Pastor Kan about myself... I simply wanted to show Pastor Kan that I was sincere. I needed acceptance from God. Pastor Kan's smile encouraged me, finally when I stopped talking, Pastor Kan suggested that since I came from a high ranking government official's family, no previous experience or family background with Christianity, I could start coming to their services on Sundays to observe, and see how that would lead me. I nodded whole-heartedly. "Yes!" I felt the acceptance from God.

Before we left, Pastor Kan also mentioned that he did not like the idea of me having an old man Mr. Fan as a friend. Pastor Kan said: "That is called *chidoufu* (eat toufu)!" Only then I realized that while I was trying to gain the acceptance from God through my bubbling, I must have mentioned my breakfast time with Mr. Fan. Oohs.

"You should not see this old man again." Pastor Kan told me, I nodded again, but this time half-heartedly. I was eager to visit their service. Somehow Pastor Kan's easy going manner convinced me that I could find God there.

On the way back, the wind stopped, the sky was blue, I felt that God was smiling at me from the above. While pedaling back leisurely, I decided that tomorrow I would tell Mr. Fan that I could not see him or eat breakfast together any more. Thus Mr. Fan was the sacrifice I offered onto the altar of God.

Chapter 19

Albert

Mr. Fan was not offended when I told him that I visited a church, and the pastor there told me that I should not see him any more. Mr. Fan was no longer among the onlookers there in the morning when I practice wushu. But his little gift was with me for quite a few years until I got married again.

Linda went with me to the church at *Chongwenmen* the following Sunday. Pastor Kan was not in the podium, it was Pastor Yin, the head of the pastor delivered the sermon. In fact, Pastor Kan seldom delivered the sermon, he was more a pastor managing the daily activities of the church.

After going to church with me twice, Linda told me that it was not for her. She preferred staying at home with my mother cooking some new dishes. I accepted her choice, I loved her cooking.

I discovered that there were bibles in English in the church! The Cultural Revolution destroyed most of the churches in China, though some of the churches were allowed to re-open after the Cultural Revolution, many of their bibles were not replaced with new ones yet. Reading a bible in English was a delight for me. Soon I was addicted to the newly discovered English study. I loved the tone when I read the verses with "thou shalt... praise thee.." I loved the stories from old Testament and stories of Jesus. From the time I discovered the bible in English, I stopped reading novels in English.

Though I left NO.156 High School, my English study continued, in my neighborhood people all knew me, the odd ball English Craze. One day there was a knock at the door at home, I opened the door, there was a girl standing at the door. "Excuse me, are you Shao-nian?" she asked, "Yes, I'm Shao-nian, please come in. What can I do for you?" I invited her in.

"My name is Lili, my friend is your sister Heping's friend, who told me that you are very good at English. I wonder if you can be my English tutor, because I make bad grade at my English." I gladly accepted Lili's request, she would pay me for my time, I did not mind earning extra money.

Lili lived in the same neighborhood. Her father was a minister of one of the Government's ministries. One day Lili came to me, she said: "Laoshi, I have one ticket for you. It is for the British Educational Equipments Exhibition. My father got it for you." I was thrilled, "Wow, this will be the first ever exhibition from a western country," I wondered, "All the exhibitions before were from Soviet Union, Romania, or Albania. Time has certainly changed!"

I eagerly anticipated the upcoming British Exhibition, "This time I will hear REAL English people talking in real time. Not from a *BBC* station on my transistor radio!"

The day came, I went to Beijing Exhibition Hall, which was next to the Zoo, it was not far from my mother's place, I got there by bicycle in less than 15 minutes, I wanted to be the first one there to get in. To my surprise, there was already hundreds of people lined up waiting to get in. 10 o'clock was the opening time, but I found out people started lining up before 7 o'clock in the morning. Everyone was eager to see the first exhibition from the West since the founding of People's Republic of China.

Beijing Exhibition Hall was built in early 60's designed by Soviet Union architects. It had tall spires, it has huge square in the front with a round fountain, with central hall, it spread to both sides with side halls. It was massive at that time. Once I got into the entrance hall, I followed the crowd and proceeded to the side hall on the left. People were everywhere, I wondered from one stand to another stand, you had to push through the crowd to get to the front to see any thing or hear anything. I almost wanted to leave, I thought to myself: "So much for hearing 'real Englishmen speaking in real time', all I could see and hear are Chinese people!"

Then I heard loud laughter from the crowd around one stand. I marched toward that crowd, I tiptoed to see what was going on by the stand, but I could not see what was happening at the stand. I ducked down, pushed, and wiggled through the crowd and stepped into the front line.

The platform of the stand was two feet high. There was an English man standing in front of a large white display board. He was bouncing from one side to the other side, talking with his hands and arms through the lady interpreter. He did not look like an average Englishman people would imagine: tall, chin up, stiff suit... he was short, with pot belly, thin curly hair, with a pair of heavy rim glasses. He looked more a comedian in a circus than an English man at education exhibition.

Now I was at the front line, my ears were ready to listen to a REAL English man talking in real time. The English man raised a pen in his hand, "Now, I am going to ask one of you," he pointed to the crowd, "to come up, and write with my magic marker on my magic board." he said. The second he finished his sentence, before the lady interpreter started translation, I raised my hand up.

The English man's face lit up when he saw my raised hand. "You understand English!" he walked toward me, "Please come up to write with my magic marker!" The English man offered me his magic marker. I jumped up to the platform, took the marker from his hand, then I walked over to the white board and started writing on the board. It was a red marker, I wrote the sentence in big letterings: Praise the Lord!

This time the English man's face was more startled. His jaw dropped a little, he paused there for a second, just when he was about to speak to me, the female government interpreter came in between me and the Englishman. She turned to me and said to me in a low but firm voice: "Please leave this stand now! No Chinese citizen was allowed to talk to a foreigner here without interpreter. Do not bring trouble to me!"

Upon hearing this, I turned to the Englishman, who was eager to know what was going on between the two Chinese ladies, I told English man in English: "Sorry sir, I should not speak to you in English here, now I'm asked to leave your stand."

The Englishman quickly pulled out a pen and his business card from his suit pocket, he swiftly wrote on his card, then handed it to me: "Come to see me at my hotel then, young lady." I left the stand under the interpreter's furiously staring. I left the crowded exhibition after that stand.

Back to my mother's place, I studied the Englishman's business card. Albert A. Stallion, Managing Director, Magiboards Ltd. He wrote the hotel and room number he was staying, with phone number. Friendship Hotel was not too far from my mother's place, 30 minutes bicycle ride. Friendship Hotel was the only hotel at the time designated as residence hotel for foreign experts living in Beijing, the hotel was walled in with army soldiers guarded with rifles at the gate!

That evening, I had to walk over to the neighborhood public phone service. I dialed the phone number of the hotel, asking for the room number. The phone was ringing at the other end. The English man answered the phone!

"Good evening, Mr. Stallion?" I asked, "This is *Youngster*, the girl who was at your stand this morning writing with your magic marker."

"Hello, how wonderful that you called!" I went on to explain to him the impossible situation of me meeting him at his hotel because of the army guards at the gate. Mr. Stallion said that he could meet me outside the hotel just cross the street, he would come out with a taxi, then I could be his guide for some sightseeing after the exhibition. It was agreed the time and the day that I would meet him as his guide

I put the phone down, the two old ladies in the phone service room gazed at me with puzzled look, they could not figure out what language I was talking on the phone. "I hope these ladies don't report to the police station of me talking English." I wondered.

That evening I told the exciting news to Linda as soon as she came back from school. "Linda, come to join me! We will talk with real English man, we will exercise our English!" Linda agreed with less enthusiasm, she doubted it could be done: Friendship Hotel? The army guards ...?

The exhibition lasted for four days, Mr. Stallion had one day free after the exhibition before he left the country. It was in winter season. I wore an old *mianhou* (translated as cotton monkey), it was a cotton padded overcoat with hood. It's faded blue color did not look right to be with the Englishman. I borrowed a fake fur-looking jacket from my sister, so that I would not look too shabby to be around with the Englishman.

The morning came, we rode our bicycles to the hotel, we parked our bicycles a little away from the hotel, and walked toward the hotel. We waited on the road side opposite the hotel. At that time, Friendship Hotel was considered in the suburbs, the road was lined up with old trees, the opposite side of the road was an open field with tall grass and trees.

We waited at the time agreed, I did not know what would happen, "Will Mr. Stallion appear at all?" My mind wandered with passing traffic flying by… suddenly a black car pulled up by our side of the road, the window rolled down, I saw Mr. Stallion's round face with his big rimmed glasses, he waved us to get into his taxi, we quickly jumped into his taxi.

"Good morning, Mr. Stallion. This is my friend Linda, she lives with my family." I said. "Good morning, girls. Just call me Albert," the English man said, "What are we going to see today?" "Summer Palace. Albert," it seemed strange, the moment I called the Englishman Albert, I felt we're same, he was not a foreign fancy Englishman any more.

The weather was good, the sun was bright, we walked along *Kunming* lake, climbed the hills, visited all the halls and gardens. Albert had a camera, he took pictures with us, he said he would have them printed and mail them to us. In the afternoon, since he had the taxi for a day, we went on to *Xiangshang* (Fragrance Hill), which was another 30 minutes away. A day passed fast, it was in winter season, the sun went down early. We decided to head back to his hotel.

Albert insisted that we should go up to his hotel room. "Chinese people are not allowed in your hotel, now can we pass those army guards at the gate?" I asked. "I have a way, just wait and I will show you." Albert promised with a smile.

Our taxi was pulling toward the gate, Albert put his hand on my shoulder, "Bend down your heads, get down in your seats!" he commanded, we did like in the army drill, ducked our heads, laying low... we went through the gate without stopping! The taxi took us straight to his room building, it was not in the main building.

We went up to his room on third floor. Once in his room, Albert opened a small fridge, he pulled out a bottle of liquor. He opened the bottle, and poured into three glasses, "Come on, ladies, cheers!" he offered to us, I hesitated for a second, I had not had alcohol since the red wine episode with Arxiao in the camp, then I took the glass, Linda followed me.

It tasted sweet and strong, it was a foreign drink, Brandy, even the name sound exotic. We sipped the liquor with Albert, chatted, from the outside winter chill changed to the warmth of a hotel room, we faces slowly turn flushed, we chatted, more brandy...

I suggested to Albert that I could try to translate his catalog into Chinese, "Most Chinese companies don't read English. If you want to open Chinese market, you need your products introduced in Chinese." I commented with enthusiasm. "Our catalogue is too technical for you to translate." Albert responded. I could see his doubt from his flushed face, "Can I have a copy of your catalogue, maybe I will try." I did not give up, Albert got up, and pulled out two or three copies of his company's catalogue from his briefcase, and handed them to me. "Of course, young lady, you can try."

We changed the subject. Until it was late, Albert ordered a taxi to his building, when the taxi came, he made sure we were inside safe, he paid the taxi driver to take us to our place.

The taxi took off. We did the same thing as the taxi approaching the gate, duck down in the seat, the taxi went through without stopping. Once outside the gate, we told the taxi driver to stop where we parked our bicycles, he was happy that he got paid and did not have to drive far at all. We jumped on our bicycles, started pedaling home, it was late, there was not much traffic at all, the road was quiet, but the ride was not as easy, I felt the same ocean wave again, I silently prayed: "Please God, keep me awake!", Linda was quiet, her bicycle wobbled too... Praise the Lord, wobbly, wobbly, we got back to my mother's apartment.

We threw our bicycles down, Linda fumbled the keys out. We stepped inside the apartment, my mother was already asleep, we tiptoed into our room, and collasped into our beds.

When I opened my eyes, it was already near noon time, the room was quiet, there was no sight of Linda, she must have left for school. I sat up in bed, "Oh, my head," I held my head with hands on my temples, it throbbed with splitting pain, "So much for the foreign brandy, though it tastes sweet. I will not touch brandy again." That was the vow, I have not touch brandy ever since.

Though intoxicated by foreign brandy, I did remember my suggestion of translating Albert's catalogue. A couple of days later, I flipped through his catalogue, I realized my common dictionary was not adequate, so I went to *Wangfujing* bookstore, the largest one in Beijing, to buy a copy of dictionary special for technology.

Beside the techno terms, I felt that translating catalogue was easier than novels. Within one month, I finished my translation. To send my translation package to England by air mail, it would cost my whole month salary! At that time I made 28 yuan, less than 3 dollars a month. I did not hesitate, though I did not promise Albert, I only volunteered, though it was under brandy's influence, Albert probably already forgot that. But I wanted to keep my words. One month salary for the postage? So be it, I would pay.

Weeks passed, one day I got a package from England! It was from Albert, there was several catalogues printed in Chinese! In his letter, Albert wrote that he received my translation, and sent them to a firm in *Hongkong* to proof. They proved it, and the result, *Magiboards* products printed Chinese.

Albert was impressed by the small Chinese woman, in his letter, he mentioned that the company planned to do more exhibitions in China, he would like to invite me to join the team, to be their exhibition's interpreter. In his letter, Albert wrote: " Please call me anytime collect, we would love to have a Chinese person work with us in China."

When I read that I smiled all over my face, I was glad that I did the translation, I sacrificed my one month salary for the postage, I was glad that my translation was proofed and printed in glossy catalogue! And finally Albert wrote that I could call England collect!

I wanted to try it, to call England, it all sounded so surreal at that time in China. To make an international call, a common Chinese had to go to one place in Beijing, the Post and Telecommunication Building, it was in downtown on

Changan Street, the widest street in Beijing at the time, it connected to *Tiananmen* Square. I rode the bicycle there, the hall for international calling was huge with 20 feet high ceiling, but few people there. Once connected, I was told to go into one of the booth.

"Hello, Miss. Shao-nian Wu?" a female voice at the other end, "Yes, I would like to talk to Mr. Stallion?" "Hold on, please." a couple of seconds, I heard Albert's voice: "Hello, my darling, have you received our package?" Albert asked.

I told him of course that was why I was calling him collect. Albert went on to tell me that they were planning to another exhibition the next year. Will I join to team. "Sure, Albert, I would be honored to join the team, but you may understand the situation in China now, no Chinese is allowed to work for a foreign firm, how could I join your team, I could be arrested at the gate of the exhibition." "I will talk to my board, we will arrange everything here for you." Albert assured me.

The talk was exuberant, I left the phone booth in high spirit, "Wow, I made a phone call all the way to England! I did not have to pay anything. Next year I may be an interpreter for an English company." I felt like a superman, only sky was the limit.

Chapter 20

China Daily

It was at the end of 1980, China was changing rapidly. I remembered that George Bush the senior, was appointed as the ambassador for China. Foreigners were allowed in our church. Occasionally when a foreigner talked to Pastor Yin after the service, if I happened to be around, Pastor Yin always asked me to be his interpreter. Thus I met Mrs. Bauer.

Mr. Bauer was the Beijing office manager of Boeing Commercial Airline. Mrs. Bauer became a regular visitor to our church. Mrs. Bauer must be in her late 50's, she had a striking appearance, though medium high, with her high heel shoes, she always appeared tall, at lease to normal Chinese people's eyes. Her hair was always blond, done in a high donut shape on top of her head, which made her seemed even taller! She always had heavy make up, brilliant red lip color.

When Mrs. Bauer found that I could speak English, she invited me to her penthouse on the top floor of Beijing Hotel. The hotel was situated right at the center of downtown, next to the biggest shopping street in Beijing at that time. Beijing hotel was often considered by foreign journalists' as their choice of stay, because of its convenient location. You can shoot news footage easily from a room window. When *Tiananmen* square shooting happened, some news photos army tanks confronted by protesters were shot up there from the rooms of Beijing hotel.

Mrs. Bauer asked me to call her Beth. She saw my sword, I always had it with me on my bicycle, because I would train wushu in the morning, then rode to church after my training. Beth asked me to show her some movements of the sword. I did it at the spacious corridor on the top floor, she was so impressed, she suggested that we should go for a real shooting outside at *Zhongshan* Park, which was not far from Beijing Hotel, just the other side of *Tiananmen* square.

So we went to *Zhongshan* park, there Beth used a whole roll of film on my sword playing. It drew a crowd watching a striking looking foreign lady with a Chinese girl playing sword, I did sword with split, toss sword in the air... Chinese people love to circle around and watch. After that, before we said good-bye, Beth invited me to join her in her Bible study group.

Beth said that their group met regularly at one of the member's apartment, which was at *Jiangoumen Wai* street. *Jiangoumen* was the section of the city where all the embassies and families resided. Of course the apartment building was in a walled compound with army soldiers at the gate.

"Youngster, if you come with me in a car, the guard will not stop you, because you could be a Japanese, or from *Hongkong*, they could not stop you as long as you're with me." Beth Bauer reassured me when I voiced me concern of venturing into diplomat's residence compound by a common Chinese.

It was in the evening, I sat with Beth Bauer at the back of the taxi. Luckily at that era, *gonganju* (Public Security Bureau) did not deploy any agents as taxi drivers, I probably would have been arrested many times as being with foreigners illegally.

The bible study was interesting, before the study, there was snack food on the table, the food flown in by Boeing from America! I was amazed to see the celery stalks three times bigger than Chinese celery. They were glad to share their American food together with faith with a common Chinese girl.

There were talks of lack of Bibles in churches in China, they wanted to contribute Bibles, but the churches were not allowed to accept anything from outside source. At the end of the study, I agreed to be the receiver for incoming Bibles, most of them would be printed in Chinese, though I emphasized that I would like to have a few copies of Bible in English version!

Mr. Bauer's position at Boeing Commercial flight, could make sure that Bibles would not get intercepted at Chinese custom, he could use diplomat channel... All was agreed. All needed was action.

A couple of weeks passed, one day after the service at the church, Beth Bauer told me that I should meet her at Beijing Hotel in the evening: there were two suitcases of Bibles arrived via Boeing. I arrived at hotel after 10 o'clock that evening, Beth was waiting for me at the lobby with two suitcases with her, we did not say much. She ordered a taxi at the reception desk, the moment the taxi pulled up in front of the gate, we got in with suitcases in the back of the car.

"Where should I take you ladies tonight?" the young taxi driver turned to me, and asked. "*Baiwanzhuang.*" I told him. "Oh, that is in the west side of the city. No problem, at this hour of the day, there should be no traffic at all." the taxi driver commented. "Yea," I nodded, and hoped that the taxi driver would not speak more.

"I hope he is not a disguised police..." I prayed while the taxi started rolling, there was a kind of excitement in the air, "Well, I am participating in an international operation!" When the taxi arrived in front of my mother's place, it was almost 11 o'clock, the street was empty, Beth waited in the taxi, the driver helped me to put two suitcases by the door of the building, off they disappeared, only empty street with dim street light.

I pushed the entrance door open, dragged two suitcases one by one inside the building, they were heavy with all the books. I dragged them into the apartment, everyone was asleep. I slowly dragged the suitcases into my room, pushed them under the bed. "Well, mission accomplished. Praised the Lord!"

Soon I realized that the mission was only partially accomplished, to get the Bibles into China, was one part, to actually distribute them was another part, and a hard part. In our church, the pastors openly told us, not to accept any materials from foreigners, even a copy of Bible. "Just politely refuse." that was what Pastor Yin and Pastor Kan told us. There was not way that I could tell them that I had two suitcases of Bibles from Americans. Certainly the Pastors did not want get into trouble. We all heard that though the church was allowed to open, there was always secret police in the congregation, to observe any activities breaking the law. Pastors wanted peace with the government.

The Americans did not want to get involved with distribution part, they could provide. I had to find my own way to distribute them. "Lord, please protect me, and direct me, let the right people come to me for these Bibles." I prayed.

Beside the Bibles, there were some devotional booklets, like *Our Daily Bread*, and books by Robert Schuller, Billy Graham. I was delighted with these books and booklets, I devoured them, they were all printed in English. I like them, because they gave me the up to date interpretation of Bible to modern daily life. Through reading them I understood Bible a lot better than simply listening to Pastor Yin's sermons in the pulpit on Sundays.

"Maybe Pastor Yin was old, maybe he was afraid to preach the real message of Bible, because of the secret police in the audience." I wondered while sitting in the pew. "I could preach this subject better than Pastor Yin." I felt the urge to speak to the audience.

One day I read an advertisement from *Beijing's Daily*, that the Central Propaganda Ministry was going to set up the first English newspaper. It would be called *China Daily*, it would be a window for the world to see what was going on in China. The advertisement was calling for all those who had the knowledge of English to participate in an open sit-in exam, to quality to work at the upcoming *China Daily*.

That was an unusual advertisement. The government never advertised jobs on newspapers. The standard scene was that when a student graduated from a college, he would then be assigned a job anywhere in China. There was no freedom to choose a job.

"Wow, this will look like the scene from the old folk tales, a scholar must take sit-in exam to be able to get an official post, all was equal before the sit-in exam." I thought, I felt the urge inside me.

I cut out the advertisement, I marked the date on my calendar. I wanted to participate, though I did not anticipate any chance for me to work at *China Daily*, I thought it would be an opportunity to test my English officially, since I was always a self-learner, no diplomas.

The date for sit-in exam for *China Daily* came. It was on a Sunday, the church service day, I did not want to miss the church service, it was my devotion to God. So I rode my bicycle to the church in the morning. I listened to Pastor Yin's sermon absent-mindedly, because my other half mind was already set to the sit-in exam.

The moment the service was finished, I didn't linger in the congregation waiting for Pastor Yin to ask me as his interpreter in case. I dashed out of the door, jumped onto my bicycle and started racing toward the sit-in exam location. Luckily the location for the sit-in was in the same city district. "Please, God, help me, don't let me miss this sit-in! Please, God, help me, don't let me miss this sit-in!" I chanted the mantra while peddling fanatically.

When I reached the location, I could see many bicycles piled outside the gate. It was an old style quadrangle courtyards. Walked inside the big roofed gate, there was a desk for registration. There were two clerks behind the desk. "Excuse me, I know that I'm late, could I still be allowed the opportunity, please!" I pleaded with absolute sincere in my eyes and tone.

The two clerks looked at each other, "This is my lifelong opportunity, please give me a chance." I urged again. The older lady said, "If you don't have enough time to complete the papers, do not blame us. It is solely your own fault for being late. Go to room No.3, there was still a seat available in the front row. Make sure that you fill all papers with your personal essentials!"

"Thank you very much!" I bowed down my head to the clerks, and run toward Room No.3 There was no sound in the quadrangle courtyard, the air of the sit-in completion was intense. I stepped inside Room No.3. There were about 40 school student desks and seats, all were occupied except the one in the middle of the front row. A few people raised their heads casting me a blaming glance, then they buried their heads down to their papers.

"Make sure that you fill all papers with your personal essentials!" I repeated the clerk's remark, and obligingly filled the personal essentials in all the papers first. I leafed through all the papers quickly: the paper for politics, "oops, this is not my strong point," I kept leafing through, the paper for Chinese literature, "not my strong point either," the paper on history, "nope, I was often caught daydreaming in history class", paper on translation from English to Chinese, "I can try this", I thought, paper on composition in English, "I can try this too."

Knowing the papers contents, and my own weakness and strength, I decided to proceed for papers on translation and composition first, in case I did not have enough time for other papers. I had not eaten anything since I got up in the morning yet, due to the rush to practice wushu then rush to church and rush to the sit-in exam. When I started writing on my papers, the hunger struck me, I reached my hand to the pocket in my jacket, pulled out a *huoshau*, (a small donut shaped baked pancake), I made a big bite into it in one hand and kept writing in another hand.

The sound of my eating *huoshau* cause small commotion, a few grumped beside and behind me, I turned my head back, it was a sea of senior folks heads, they wore reading glasses, they must be language professionals from other government institutes. I could see their disapproval of a young girl eating *huoshau* in the grand sit-in exam for *China Daily*!

I stopped chewing, I felt not only their disapproval of my eating *huoshau*, but their superiority of their knowledge. I turned my head back, and down, "I don't have any chance with these senior translators." I thought. Right then I decided that I would forfeit my attempt, I would only fill the paper on translation and composition, just a test for myself, as for the rest papers I would leave them blank.

Once that decision made, I proceeded finishing my small *huoshau* and my selected papers, When I finished two papers, I stood up, I walked toward the door, I saw the shock from those seniors contenders eyes: "This young girl, last one walked in, eating *huoshau* in the exam, and now the first one walked out ..." Some of them shook their heads, it was clear that they did not approve my defiance to the grand sit-in.

I walked out of the gate of the quadrangle courtyard, left the two clerks behind the desk with puzzled looks on their faces.

Three weeks passed, I forgot the sit-in exam experience, then one day I got a mail, it was from *China Daily*. The letter informed me that I was scheduled for an interview at *China Daily*'s office! That was a shock to me, I did not complete all the papers, I left them blank...

I went to *China Daily*'s office, it was across the town, at east side. The huge compound was guarded with armed soldiers at the gate. *China Daily* at that time shared the compound with *People's Daily*, the No.1 government newspaper.

Once inside the huge compound, I followed the instruction and found *China Daily's* office building, it was a new building of two story high along the eastern wall of the compound. The interview at the Human Resource Dept. was not hard, they asked some routine questions. They told me that I did well with translation and composition, regardless of my blank papers on politics, history and Chinese literature.

Three days later, I heard the postman called out my name outside the apartment building, I went out, the postman handed me a letter for me to sign. It was from *China Daily*, I eagerly opened the letter, there was the exciting news that I was officially hired to work at *China Daily*! Their HR department would do all the work transfer paper, I only had to report to work at *China Daily* on next Monday.

It all happened fast, I rode to the Steel Plant to complete the transfer paper, the older workers at my sweeping team commented that they all knew that I would not stay there with them long, with my odd English papers everyday, and fancy color photos of my playing sword in *Zhongshan* park, that was the first time they saw someone had color photos taken, simply put as they said that I did not belong there.

My mother was overjoyed by my work transfer to the prestige coveted work place like *China Daily*, I was glad too to see that I could make my mother smile proudly again, I had felt sorry that my mother had to bear a shame because of my divorce. Though I did not know what I would be assigned to work at *China Daily* yet, I was ready to do my best, no matter what kind of work.

That night I laid in my bed, "I cannot imagine that I will work among those senior editors, and reporters at the first ever English newspaper in China. Praise the Lord! This is a miracle." with this sweet feelings, slowly I drifted into my sleep.

Chapter 21

A Zealot

China Daily was at the east side of the city, I lived at the west side, it was not safe to ride through all the traffic over long distance. I decided to travel by bus, but sometimes it took two hours to get to work. I found out that I could stay at the office for the night, if I had my sleeping pad. That solved the problem of wasting time traveling through the city to work at China Daily. I would stay at the office after work. My early morning wushu practice had to stop, though often I practiced it in the yard in front of *China Daily*'s building..

I was assigned to work at typesetting room. *China Daily* installed the latest news publishing system imported from Australia. Mr. Jones, the Australian was often at the typesetting room teaching us how to use the system. There were Ted and Judy from America working with editors, reporters. The original team was small, altogether less than 50 which including all the supporting staffs from security to logistics and HR.

With small team, it was more like a family, Chief Editor and assistant editors knew everyone by first name. Many of them call me *Youngster*. I was glad that I could work in an environment that English was a necessary work skill, it was not considered as a negative element. I would talk in English when it was possible at work. To my astonishment that was not normal. From Chief Editor down to all editors, reporters, they seldom talk in English. They would converse in Chinese, though they wrote and read in English as work.

I was young, I did not have degree or diploma, I did not have "a face to lose" if I made mistakes in speaking English, so soon I became known at the *Daily* that "Youngster could SPEAK in English"! Though I was working at Typesetting room, often editors or reporters would come to me to talk in English.

About a month passed after I arrived at *China Daily*, the celebration of Chinese New Year was held upstairs at the Meeting Room next to Chief Editor's office. It was an afternoon, instead of working, everyone was invited to the party to celebrate the New Year and get to know each other at the *Daily*. All the tables were pushed onto one side of the room, there were plates loaded with wrapped candies, roasted sunflower seeds, oranges, and apples on the tables, plus several hot water flasks filled with jasmine tea.

The atmosphere was relaxed, we all stood around, chatting, cracking sun flowers, laughing waiting for the Chief Editor to make the speech. Soon the Daily's Manager Zhang announced: "Hello, attention, everyone! Today after the Chief's speech, we would have a singing party! Everyone in the room will sing, in turns!" We all looked at each other, someone in the crowd shouted: "Manager Zhang leads first!", the crowd cheered with clapping hands. I was standing in the front line, not too far from Manager Zhang, after he finished a song, he passed the microphone to the next person, soon the mike was in the hands of the person standing next to me, though I knew I did not sing well, I was not afraid of singing in the public, but what song? People were singing the popular songs, I had to think a song when my turn came, in minutes!

The mike phone was in my hand, I said: "If I have to sing in front of others, here is my song to praise my Heavenly Father." I started singing a hymn song I learned in the church ... the crowd went quiet, before I could finished the song, Manager Zhang pulled the HR officer outside the room shouted to him: " How did you people recruited a Christian in here?"

The singing party continued, when the party finished, I trailed with crowd walking downstairs, Chief Editor's assistant, a tall man in his 40's following me behind, "Hey, *Youngster*!" he said in a low voice, "Is it possible that you get me a copy of Bible?" I looked up at his face, I could see his sincereness through his thick rimmed glasses. I quietly nodded, he gave me back a smile.

Back to the office, everyone was getting to leave, a lady editor Wang Yan in her 30's came to the office, after looking around, waiting for others to leave, she asked me: "Hello, *Youngster*, could you get me a copy of Bible?" then she paused for a couple of seconds, "Is it possible that you take me to your church for a service?" she added.

I took Wang Yan to our church the following Sunday, eventually she was baptized in the church.

After the Chinese New Year's holiday, I returned to work that morning, as soon as I walked into the building, I was told to see the Manager Zhang upstairs. I walked into his office, there beside Manager Zhang's desk, sat the security office too. Manager Zhang started: "Wu Shao-nian, how come that you did not tell us that you are a Christian when we gave you the interview?"

"I was never asked?", I calmly replied. Religion was not an issue at that time in China, almost everyone was an atheist assumed.

"In that case," Manager Zhang retorted, "We give you three days to consider of changing your choice of religion. You know this is a governmental propaganda department to the world, we do not want any Christian working here!"

Three days later, I was ordered to report to Manager Zhang's office. "Tell us what is your decision?" Manger Zhang did not waste time when I entered his office. I did not want to waste his time either.

"Christianity is important to me as a personal choice. It does not interfere my work here, I choose not to change it." I told Manager Zhang as a matter of fact.

Manager Zhang seemed prepared for my decision, "In that case," he said in a business matter, "We choose to remove you from Typesetting office! It is an important place at *China Daily*, we simply cannot have a Christian there! From today you will move downstairs to the reference room."

"All right, so be it. I will move to the Reference Room downstairs. Anything else?" I said without any emotion. I was not upset by the animosity of Manager Zhang's decision, after all he was doing what he was trained to do.

Working in Reference Room was less demanding, there was no deadlines to finish. Most times the reference was quiet, only one or two editors coming in looking for a particular piece of information, and we were there to assist.

My daily routine was to file information into different categories, though we had the latest publishing line from Australia, it was not integrated together with all departments. We file all the information by paper, glue, file holders and cutters. It was all reading, cutting, clipping, pasting ... What a quantum leap comparing the methods of filing information nowadays, paperless and instant!

I liked my work at *China Daily*, because it involved English language! I no longer read my English articles audibly in the morning in my mother's garden, I no longer made time to study English, my work was my study, all the information I filed was in English, I read it and filed it. Now I devoted my spare time to religion instead of English.

The pastors organized Youth Fellowship, quite a few young, and new members joined the activities. I, of course, joined it eagerly. Our Youth Fellowship was just social gathering, I was a little bit disappointed. One day, I asked Pastor Kan: " Kan Mushi, Can we have bible study during our Youth Fellowship?" Pastor Kan said, "That is not necessary, don't we have Sunday service for bible study?"

I was a little discouraged by Pastor Kan's remarks. After talking to a few young members at the Youth Fellowship, they all expressed the need to study bible together. I started my own bible study group outside the church without telling pastors, they would not prove it anyway. Through my studying of books smuggled through Mrs. Bauer, I felt the urge to share the knowledge which the pastors would not preach in the pulpit.

One day after the service, a tall young man approached. "Hello, Miss, my name is Robin. I saw that you were reading a Bible in English during the service." We started chatting. Robin was a student at Beijing Language College. He came from England. He said he was very impressed to see young Chinese people in our church.

"We have a Youth Bible Study group, would you like to join us?" I eagerly invited him, "Don't tell our pastors, they would not like it. We meet outside the church." I cautioned him.

Robin's face lit up, "Of course, I would be so delighted." he said in a lower voice, he went on to explain, "When I was in Hongkong, I worked with a group of Christian youth there, if you don't mind, I can prepare some study material and share with the group."

My almost jumped with joy, "Wow, we will be very happy to hear how young Christians in *Hongkong* studying Bible." We decided that next Sunday after the service, I would arrange my group to meet Robin for a bible study gathering.

Everyone of my group was excited for the upcoming gathering with Robin, a student from England! The following Sunday after the service, we all left the church fast, we gathered outside the church around the street corner so that the pastors could not see us together with Robin. Robin suggested that we could go to the coffee shop in *Wangfujing* street. "It will be my treat for everyone!"

The Coffee Shop was opened recently. Drinking coffee was a novelty at that time. The shop was not busy, the deco was modern, clean, especially the music in the background, it was different! It was definite not the familiar tunes of the revolutionary songs we heard from Radio. When we saw the price for a cup of coffee, we all looked at each other: it was expensive for us.

Robin said, "Please don't worry about the price, it is my day, I am so happy to be with all you here. We are here to study Bible!"

We all settled down into two booths next to each other, Robin ordered coffee for all of us, the warm air of the Coffee

Shop mixed with exotic coffee aroma made us relaxed and at the same time excited, and the music ...

When we asked the man behind the service counter, what was the music he was playing, "It is the latest songs from *Hongkong*!" the owner proudly held up the cover of the cassette to show us.

Robin smiled, he took a cassettes from his backpack! "I have the music from Hongkong too." he got up and walked over to the service counter.

"Ni keyi ting zhege yinyue (Which means you can play this music)," Robin surprised the shop owner with his Chinese though not perfect with the tone, "Ye shi Xianggang de (which means it's also from *Hongkong*)."

The owner said, "Great, let us all hear it." he took the cassette, had a look at the cover, but it was in English, "Yingwen de? Hey, genhao (which means In English? Even better)."

The music drifted in the coffee shop, the tempo changed from pop to relaxed, "Jesus, You're my morning star...." though only Robin and me In the coffee shop understood the lyrics, people's chatting noise lowered, everyone in the coffee shop seemed noticed or affected by the music.

"I cannot not believe it. Here I am sitting in a coffee shop in No.1 shopping street with Chinese Christian youth, and we are listening to the Christian music with public!" Robin said with his hands spread out and eyes scanned the whole shop.

Robin went on to lead our group with Bible study, every member of the group was glad for the experience of youth fellowship with someone from different part of the world. We all agreed that we would continue to study Bible with Robin when he had time.

Robin later on even enlisted more foreign students from Beijing Language College to have fellowship with us young Christians in Beijing. Later on his girlfriend Lucy from England too. Lucy was a beautiful redhead girl. Always ready to smile. All these foreign students could speak some Chinese. On the Christmas Day that year, we all gathered together at one member's, it was a memorable evening, I still had a couple of photos Robin took at the Christmas gathering.

One day, we had our Bible study gathering in *Zhongshan* park, since it was in the middle of the city, half way for people to come from any side of the city, east or west. The park is beautiful, plenty old pine trees. There were about six of us, we sat down at a quiet spot, I gave them each a copy of Bible, so that they could read and take home. I prepared that day's study topics, we read the bible, they made notes on which verses in the New Testaments to study. The sounds of children playing nearby gradually faded away, we were engrossed in our study and discussion... time went fast.

The sun was setting, I concluded the study, we all said good-by to each other and left the park through different gates. Later in the evening, I heard a knock at the door at home, when I opened the door, there was *Li Jianan*'s mother standing by the door!

Li Jianan was a member of my bible study group, he came from a Christian family, I saw his mother often at the service at the church. *Li Jianan* was a few years younger than me, I was older than most of the members in our Bible study group. They all looked up to me, I led the group, I had the connection from abroad, I could supply Bibles, if they needed them for their friends, I could speak English, I was brave...

Li Jianan was a quiet spoken young man, slim, medium height, pale complexion, always had a small mustache, the mustache would add some masculinity to his frail figure. Though quiet, I could always feel his support to my group, he called me "Shaonian Jie", which meant "sister". We were very close, many years later, though I left China, I occasionally heard from him, of his marriage, his mother's pass away, he eventually became a pastor in our church in Beijing!

"Hello, auntie?" I greeted her with question in my mind, "Was Jianan with you this afternoon for bible study?" his mother asked. "He was still not home yet!" she added.

"What?" I was shocked by the fact that Li Jianan was not home, "We finished the study after 5 o'clock. We left Zhongshan park after that, but he left by another gate." I told auntie. By then my mother came to ask what was going on. We were all puzzled by Li Jianan's disappearance.

"I told you not to do this bible study thing! But you just don't listen." my mother was always ready to blame me for anything gone wrong.

But none of us could come with any explanation, this was not like *Li Jianan*, he was a man of consideration. *Li Jianan* lost his father during the Cultural Revolution, he never mentioned why and how. He was the youngest child, now living with his mother. He was always gentle, he could never do this to his mother by going somewhere late without telling her.

It was getting late, my mother suggested that I should accompany Li Jianan's mother home. "Don't miss the last bus, go now, maybe Li Jianan is at home now." my mother urged us.

I went with auntie back to her apartment, which was at the east side of the city. We waited, eventually, I fell asleep in their couch in the living room… "Jianan! You're back." I was awaken by auntie's voice. I looked up, here standing in the middle of the room was Li Jianan. Tired, by otherwise composed. It was already five o'clock in the morning.

"What happened to you? Jianan!" auntie demanded with concern. "I was at the police station. Mom. But don't worry, everything is alright." *Li Jianan* answered her with his usual quiet voice.

Li went on to tell us the whole story. When we were studying bible in Zhongshan Park, we did not know that our group activity caused park security's attention, a secret police was assigned to keep surveillance on us. When we left the park in different directions, he arrested Li Jianan at the other gate, and took him to the police station.

They kept him overnight, due to the lack of any evidence, they could not persecute him for just reading Bible with a group, Bible was the only thing they found on him. The government was telling the world that it allowed religion freedom by then.

"I am not opposing you young people studying bible, but please do not ever study bible in the public!" auntie said, though she was talking to *Li Jianan*, I knew that she was telling me as well.

"You can all come to my place to study." Auntie said, "Really, auntie?" I wanted to confirm her offer. "Yes. Come here, though our apartment is small, but it will not get you all into trouble again with police." *Li Jianan*' mother said with determination. From then on, we no longer held our Bible study outside in the public place, we had a "home" for our group.

One day while I was walking on a street near home, a young man came right up to me, "Could you give me a copy of bible?" he asked me. I was surprised, "Is he a secret police?" I wondered. "Please, Lord, guide me, protect me." I prayed silently.

"Who are you? Why do you ask me for a copy of bible?" I demanded in a quiet but firm voice.

"I saw you at the church when they presented musical *Messiah*, you were with choir, you were at the front line. I remembered your face!" the young man answered my questions.

He did not give me time to asses his truthfulness. He continued, "That day I went to your church with my elder brother. He is a student at Beijing University ..." the young volunteered more information for me.

"My brother told me that there was a lecture on world religion one day at the campus. It drew a huge audience, there were no seats left, many had to listen to it outside through windows! That had never happened in campus' history!" the young man continued, "We want to know more on Christianity, but there is no Bible available anywhere. Even in the church, you can not ask for a copy of Bible."

I knew he was right, there was no printing house in China then allowed to print Bible, the churches did not have enough Bible for service. I was moved by his story at the campus of Beijing University. "Please follow me then, I will help you get a copy of Bible."

The young man waited outside my mother's apartment building. I came out with a copy of Bible. He was delighted, with his hands feeling over the cover of the bible, he looked up into my eyes, "This is for my brother. Can I have one copy for myself too? Please." he said sheepishly.

When the young man walked away with two copies of Bibles in his hands, I prayed that they would land in the rightful hands. No police knocked at my mother's apartment door afterwards. Praise the Lord!

Through my Bible study group members, we distributed most of the bibles to villages in the rural area, even *Li Jianan*'s mother helped us. The rural villages did not have any resource for the Bible. When I finally left China in 1984, only 4 copies of Bible left at home, my mother eventually gave them to others. Though she was not a Christian, she told me that she read Bible too, when I was not around! She said that she liked the stories in the Bible.

"I like the young people in your group when they are here." my mother later commented, "They are good mannered, and polite people."

Chapter 22

A Free Bird

It was about summer of 1982, work at the Reference Room at *China Daily* became a routine, the shock of my Christian identity at the Daily was faded, I never tried to convert any one at *China Daily*. My bible study activity was strictly with youth fellowship members from the church. I was just *Wu Shaonian*, pasting and filing quietly by my desk at the Reference Room. No one approached me for another copy of Bible. I did not take another staff from *China Daily* to the church.

It seemed all forgotten, except Manager Zhang. One day in the late morning, when I went to Ladies toilet on the ground floor, here was water everywhere, the mini flood even flew to the corridor. People simply stepping over or hopping over flood water to get anywhere. I found a broom, a bucket and a mop and started cleaning up the water from corridor toward the toilet.

Suddenly Manager Zhang appeared from nowhere, seeing me on my knees on the floor collecting and dumping water into the bucket, he stood afar and shouted: "Where are others? Where are the communist party members? How can we let a Christian win here by doing this!" His strange anger at me quickly reminded me that they had not forgotten that they did not want a Christian at a government's propaganda organization.

One Sunday after the service at the church, an old lady with all grey hair and crinkles all over her face approached me in the ial, "Hey, you are Wu Shao-nian, aren't you?" she wanted to confirm her statement, "I heard that you can speak English, I have a man from America, could you translate for me, please?", she did not wait for me to reply, she simply walked away.

When she returned there was the American apparently in his 50's trailing behind her. His hair was all grey just like the old lady, but fewer rinkles on his broad face, with grey beard all around his lower jaw, a pair of rimless spectacles. His body certainly matched his face, broad, round, but his appearance did not make his appearance fat, only strong. He supported an air of authority.

"Hello," the American stepped forward with his hand extended to me, "I am Dr. Kennedy, I am here today with my Chinese friend to have service together in your church."

"Hello, Dr. Kennedy. I am Wu Shaonian. Your friend asked me to be the translator for you, I hope I can be a help." I politely received his hand and greeted back.

"Woo Shoo nanny.." Dr. Kennedy fumbled with my name, the old lady and I could not help but giggled at his struggle, then Dr. Kennedy waved his hands in the air to signal that he gave up pronouncing my name correctly.

"Miss, can I call you Maria? This will be easy for me." Dr. Kennedy looked into my eyes, almost begging me to help by accepting his name for me.

"Maria?" I hesitated with the sound, "it certainly sounds softer than *Youngster*," I thought. "Alright, Dr. Kennedy. You can call me Maria." I consented with a sense of anticipation of something new will come into my life with my new English name. The old lady with grey hair asked me to call her Yang Nainai (Granny Yang). She was the caretaker of an apartment which belonged to Dr. Kennedy's friend in California. Thus was the thread that formed web which connected us all together.

Dr. Kennedy apparently was impressed by my interpretation skill between him and Yang Nainai. "Maria," he asked before they left the church, "Is it possible that you can accompany me to a meeting tomorrow morning? I can really use an interpreter for the meeting!"

"Humm...." it all happened so fast, "Tomorrow I have to work at *China Daily*. But I certainly would love the opportunity to be Dr. Kennedy's interpreter, what will be an special experience!" My mind was racing.

"OK, Dr. Kennedy, it will be an honor to work for you tomorrow." I took the invitation.

"I have to get another sick leave note for tomorrow!" My mind was made.

I met Dr. Kennedy at his room at Beijing Hotel, it was early, Dr. Kennedy took me to eat breakfast buffet at the hotel's dinner hall. The sight of the food was a feast itself, for a common Chinese girl like me at the time. The dining hall was big with high ceiling, gold motif everywhere, soft red carpet, soft music, there were only a handful of people eating at that early hours.

The food was served in both Western and Chinese style: toast, French toast, jam, sausage, juice. *Xifan* (rice porridge), *pidan* (fermented egg), *baozi* (steamed dumpling)

... the food seemed went on and on, I felt like Alice in the Wonderland, trying to take all that in: the sight, the scent, the sound, the feel ...

Suddenly I heard my name is called out "*Youngster*!" I looked to the direction of the sound, there Beth Bauer was sitting by a table having her breakfast alone. I went over to her table, Dr. Kennedy found me there soon and we all sat down with Beth for the breakfast together.

Through Dr. Kennedy and Beth's conversation I learned more about Dr. Kennedy. He was the president of *US-China Education Foundation* based in North Carolina. His *Foundation* was probably the first of the very few cultural programs from US granted by the Chinese government at that time. He frequently flew to China for the talks between government, universities and airlines.

After the breakfast I went with Dr. Kennedy to a printing factory which was very close to my mother's place! Dr. Kenney wanted to have over 3,000 copies of a letter printed, and envelopes with Foundation's logo. He wanted to mail *Foundation*'s letter to all the universities in the US about the Foundation's Chinese language program, short term and long term program.

Dr. Kennedy had only three days in Beijing, during those three days, beside working at the Daily, I spent most of my free time being with him, with other meeting, or going around Beijing, even shopping. 3 days together must gave him enough time to assess my integrity. before he left China, he asked me to help finalizing the *China Mail* project. Dr. Kennedy left me with enough money to pay for the printing and purchasing envelops, stamps. I never had that much money in my hands before. I was a little rich Chinese girl! Though I did not tell anyone.

I went back to the printing factory several times, to proof the final print. When 3,000 copies of letters printed, I followed Dr. Kennedy's instruction: I bought colorful stamps, addressing to all the universities from a big thick US Universities Directory by hand. Dr. Kennedy said he liked the idea that the letters were went from China, with bright colorful stamps to get the attention of the university people there in US.

Early summer in 1982, I received a letter from England, it was from *Magiboards Limited*. They informed me that the company would participate the upcoming second British Trade Exhibition that summer. They would like to hire me as the company's own interpreter, because I translated his catalogue, I had enough about their product.

I was thrilled: "Work for a foreign company? This is never heard of in China while I grew up!" my spirit was sky high, but my mind quickly brought me back to the reality: "But of course it is illegal for a Chinese citizen working for a foreign company!" I have seen and heard during the cultural Revolution so many people with any foreign connections were persecuted, head shaved, paraded in the street, or in prison... my mind swiftly returned to the scene of *Jin Zheng* dragging me to the police station to report me for listening to BBC ...

That night I rode my bicycle to the *Central Telecommunication Building* in downtown, I called collect to England. The secretary Olga put me through to their Chairman, "Hello, Albert," I greeted him, "I received the company's invitation for me. Thank you. But I worry because it is illegal for a Chinese working for you." I explained to him.

"*Youngster*, I understand this, I will discuss this at our next board meeting, we will inform you soon of what we can do to protect you." Albert spoke on the phone with assurance.

I called Albert again a week later, he told me they will prepare an official ID for me, it would look like a passport, they had photos of me from Albert's last trip to China. "What name should we put on the ID book?" Albert asked, I thought for a moment: "Not Wu Shao-nian, that will definitely cause attention as a local Chinese. *Youngster?* That does not sound like a real English name. Maria Woo? Yes, Maria Woo! It sounds like an oversea Chinese name. It will be a good protection for me."

Magiboards Ltd. would book their team hotel rooms together through 48 Group, which was under the British Trade Commerce, that would include a room for me by *Maria Woo*. All I need to do was to show up at the airport, then from there I would be with British group throughout the Exhibition. I would be one of them.

Albert mentioned that I did not even need a suitcase, "We would come with your suitcase too, with your clothes too. You should dress like a member from a British team!"

After the phone call to England, I was determined that I would join Albert's exhibition team. I could no think of upcoming event of British Exhibition with me disguising as one of the. "Will the security or police recognize me, and arrest me?" It felt like a spy mission, the thought made my heart beat faster ... I chose not to think about it too much, otherwise I would forfeit the opportunity. I dare not tell anyone, because they would certainly talk me out of it. It was just unheard of any Chinese doing it!

The second British Trade Exhibition would be running in Tienjin, a major port city about 100 miles away from Beijing. It would be a three day exhibition. Plus time for travel to and back to Beijing, I would need 5 days off from work. "How do I get five days off from work? Of course a sick leave note from a doctor!" My mind worked hard.

The only physical problem I could remember since childhood was gum disease, periodontal. I could see a dentist, a look at my gum he would see I am a legitimate patient, if only I could get my temperature up, then I could ask for a sick note.

I practiced a few times inserting a thermometer into a hot *mantou* (steamed bun) to have perfect readings, not too hot otherwise I would fail to secure a sick note. Soon I was ready for the day when I should go to the airport to meet *Magiboards*'s team.

The day came, I went to see a dentist in the small clinic just across the street from my mother's apartment, that was convenient. With a warm *mantou* wrapped in a small towel hidden in my pocket. I did not have problem to have the temperature up. All went well, I got a sick note.

At the last moment before I left for the airport, I told my mother that I will be working as an interpreter for the British company in Tienjing for 3 days. She was surprised, "How can you ..." she said, but I did not give her time to think more or talk more, "Mom, I am late, I have to run, I will be back." I run out of the door.

After long bus ride to Beijing Capital Airport, (at that time, it would take more than one hour to get to the airport, now with expressway, only 20 minutes), I found the way to the International Arrival hall, it was my first time at an airport!

When their flight finally arrived, when the Westerners walked out of the gate, I spotted Albert's pot belly figurer right away, trailing behind him was a tall, handsome young man in a dark business suit. Albert saw me too. "Hello, Maria Woo!" Albert pronounced my English name loud and clear with a big grin on his face.

I smiled back at him too. "Maria Woo, here the mission starts. Lord, please be on my side, protect me." I prayed silently.

Albert stepped aside waving his open palm toward the handsome young man behind him, "Please meet our team member Brian." he said.

The handsome young man stepped forward and reached out his hand, "Hello, Maria, nice to meet you." Brian was at least 6 feet tall, light brown skinned, he had thick long wavy dark hair, like those Beatle boy's style, his big eyes were deep set but with warm glow. He had an inviting smile on his lips too. Thus the 3-member *Magiboards* Ltd team formed at Beijing Airport.

Albert pulled out a small black suitcase from his luggage cart, "This is for me, Maria." he said, and pushed it toward me. It was a nice smooth leather suitcase from *Burberry*, London. Slim small enough to be allowed to carry on the plane.

"Ok, now let's look for the rest of the group." We found the them further down in the hall, there the government receiving personnel led us to a big coach bus, the bus took us to Beijing Railway Station. Stepping off the coach, we followed the government guide to the VIP lounge, I realized that people all stared at us, a group of Laowai (foreigner), I had to play my role as *Maria Woo* well.

The train ride to *Tienjin* was less than two hours, at *Tienjin* railway station another bus took us straight to the hotel. I did not have to do anything at all at the reception desk, Brian and I waited in a sofa down the hall, Albert returned with keys for three rooms for each of us. Albert told us that we only had a couple of hours to rest, then we would head for the exhibition hall to setup the stand. All the items for the exhibition had already arrived there.

Once in my room, I opened the sleek leather suitcase, I pulled out an overcoat, deep wine color, the lining was beige Scottish tartan design, it was from Burberry, London, I tried it on, it fit me perfect! There was a floral skirt, two blouses, a white nylon pants with bell bottom, the cut, the style, the material, the prints, were definitely foreign. I changed into one blouse and with white pants, standing in front of a big mirror: I looked like a lady from *Hongkong*, Maria Woo was the right name for the role.

We went to the exhibition hall in the afternoon, Brian was skillful at setting up the display stand, with three of us, the stand was ready for tomorrow's show. Brian was not only quick at work, he was quick at cracking jokes too, he was funny! He put his palm over my head, and then leveled it with his shoulder, "Maria, you are so small, let me call you *Grasshopper*, please?" he asked with smiling eyes. Thus I got a new nickname from Brian.

Three days in *Tienjin* passed fast, everyday, we got up, quick breakfast, with bus to the exhibition hall, standing at the display stand, answering questions when asked. Albert and Brian were all professionals at showing their products, both of them had good salesmanship, they were certainly not the stereotype of arrogant English men, when they talked with people. they tried to make people laugh.. .Albert called it kidology: kidding with customers, make them relaxed, form a rapport, then seal the deal.

We did not have any time to go anywhere in *Tienjin*. During three days at the exhibition, we only traveled from hotel to the exhibition and back to hotel. I did not have any memory of *Tienjin* as a city at all. There was no one suspected me being a local Chinese mingled with Brits at the exhibition. I was treated just like a *laowai*. Three days working with Albert and Brian definitely improved my ability as an interpreter, and relationship with Albert and Brian, we really worked like a team, their *kidology* certainly worked on me, I was a laughing *Grasshopper* every day.

When the exhibition finished, the three member *Magiboards* team traveled back to Beijing, Albert told me that he would like to invite my family for a dinner that evening at Jianguo Hotel, where they checked in.

I ordered a taxi home, the driver greeted me with politeness, treating me like a foreigner, I found myself spoke Chinese with faked southern accent, I might as well play as Maria Woo to the end.

My mother was relieved seeing me back from *Tienjin*. "*Shao-nian*, I worried about you to death for three days! How can you have such big guts? Aren't you afraid that they will arrest you for having liaison with foreigners?" she greeted me with her barrage of remarks.

"Mom, can't you see I am all right. I am back sound and safe." I replied calmly. I told her that Albert invited everyone for a dinner at *Jianguo* hotel.

She was shocked first, then she pulled the edge of her blouse and asked sheepishly: "Should I go like this?" "Of course, Mom. Albert and Brian are easy people. You should go to have a look at *Jianguo* hotel." I assured her.

That evening, my mom, me and my brother went to Jianguo hotel. The hotel was the newest four star hotel recently completed. It was situated near diplomatic area. Beside Beijing hotel and Friendship Hotel, it was the third hotel where foreigners could stay, it was the highest standard at that time, built by foreign hotel chain for foreign businessmen visiting China. It was the first Western hotel.

The solemn door man outside at the entrance looked smart with red tailed suits and gold trims on his shoulder pads and cap. Many local onlookers stood afar, I led my mother, brother, marching forward toward the entrance, Under my Western clothes, my confident manner, the door man stepped on the side waving his palm and gave way to us, no question asked. Three days working with Albert and Brian at Tianjin made me assured with role of Maria Woo. I realized as long as I dressed right, spoke right (English, and accented Chinese), with an assured manner, no local police or security would dare to stop me. I also had a little "passport" stating that I was a staff from *Magiboards* Ltd. in England.

Stepping inside the lobby, everywhere you looked, it boasted Western luxury, from the design, the furnishing, a pianist was playing some soft classical melody, it almost felt surreal from the post *Cultural Revolution* atmosphere outside the hotel.

I called Albert's room number from the lobby, when Albert and Brian walked out of the elevator toward us, it was a funny sight: Brian, a tall, handsome, young man and Albert, a short, pot-belly, thin hair bald headed man with big rim glasses, his big feet seemed bigger than his height in proportion. Albert's walking manner was with his big feet slight pointing outward. With their *kidology* grin, they could be the British circus clowns invading China.

Albert led us to a restaurant just across from the lobby. It was the only one opened at that time. Later on, there were more restaurants open in Jianguo, a Chinese, a Japanese. The restaurant was dim lighted, the deep red tone velvet curtains were running from ceiling to the floor, the candles on the tables were flickering, we were seated down by a round table. When I looked at the menu, it was all Western cuisine, the price was astronomical, "I bet that Robin could not afford eating here." I thought.

Albert asked my mother and brother what they would like to order, he wanted to treat them a good Western meal. My mother told him that he could order what he thought the best for them. Albert ordered the best from the menu: (Air Flown) New Zealand sirloin steak for all of us and steak tartar for himself.

There were few people dining at the restaurant, the price was simply not for ordinary people, especially in that era. The food arrived, served on a hot big flat plate with big sizzling charred steak placed in front of my mom, me and my brother. Brian ordered same steak. The sight of the steak made him grinned, "Oh, thank God, finally I can have a steak!" Three days in *Tienjin* made him sick of Chinese porridge, rice, stir fries.

Albert and Brian looked at us, our hands were on our laps, they waited for us picking up the forks and knives, but we simply stared at the big chunk of charred New Zealand steak. We could not eat it, we did not know how to, the sight of it was simply too much a shock to swallow.

We all went through 60s famine, and the Cultural Revolution. When we went to buy meat at the market, we would usually buy a slice of it for ten cents, that would be a meal for a whole family, it would be cut into small threads, stir-fried with a lot of vegetable. Occasionally, we would buy 50 cents of meat to cook as a stew, on festivals, maybe one *yuan* of meat for cook several different dishes the whole family. At that time one dollar equaled almost ten *yuan*!

Looking at the gigantic charred meat, it's like looking at a butcher's counter, we simply could not stomach it. Albert apologized for not understanding the culture difference. Brian said that he could handle another plate of steak for us.

Be the end we ate all the vegetables from the plate, Brian managed to finish three pieces of steak! My family enjoyed the desert, the fancy Ice cream Alaska with live flame in the bowl ignited by a waiter right in front of our eyes! After diner, Albert and Brian walked us out of the hotel, the next day they would fly back. Albert ordered a taxi for us, when the taxi pulled up, Albert turned to me: "Maria, I will come back soon." then he turned to my mom: "Good bye, Mama, I will see you again, I promise next time, I will order Chinese food for you." When I translated it to mom, we all had a hearty laugh.

The following day, I went to work at *China Daily*, when I handed my sick note to *Zhao Xiaoliang*, the head of the

Reference Room, he smiled and gave me a funny look. I did not say a word any more. It would be worse trying to explain a lie. The policy "Don't ask and don't tell" worked here. My three days whirlwind experience as *Maria Woo* changed me, I became bolder, equipped with western clothes, *Magiboards Ltd.* Passport, the calm manner, I thought that I could fool the local security people and the police.

Soon after Albert left Beijing, I got a telex that Dr. Kennedy would arrive in Beijing, and staying at *Jianguo* hotel. *Jianguo* was the hottest hotel in town if you could afford it. After work, I went to Jianguo, and met Dr. Kennedy and his young secretary Denise at the lobby. I went upstairs with them to his room.

"Maria, these are for you." Dr. Kennedy handed me a big bag, when I opened it, there were clothes in it: one long orange-browning leather overcoat, and a purple woolen dress. They were beautiful and luxurious. Looking into my bewildered eyes, he explained: "I hope with these clothes, it will be easier for you to be with us. I can always bring you more clothes if you need."

I looked around his room, it was turned into an office, there was a typewriter on the desk, and papers, files, and his suitcases. Dr. Kennedy and Albert were definitely different. Albert always traveled light, a briefcase, a small carry on suitcase. That was it. Albert's room was always in order, neat and tide, he did not carry a lot of paperwork, all was handled by telex. But Dr. Kennedy traveled with lots of stuff. He even carried all those tiny soap bars from previous hotels! In his room, there were always papers spilled all over the desk, bed, floor...and oversized suitcases, big thick briefcase like those for the lawyers, plus big zippered carry on bag with shoulder strips, like for those pro football players.

Dr. Kennedy told me that this time Denise would train me on how to work for *US-China Education Foundation*: how to use typewriter, how to work with different Chinese government offices. I started calling Dr. Kennedy: *Doc* as Denise did.

During their two weeks staying in Beijing, I spent most of my free time with them, plus a couple of sick leave notes I managed to present to *Zhao Xiaoliang*, my office head boss, I learned a lot. People at Foreign Affairs Office at Beijing University, Beijing Ethnic College all thought that I was with Dr. Kennedy's Foundation from outside China, I perfected my Chinese with Hongkong accent. People working at the Front Desk at Jianguo Hotel all knew my face because I was there everyday in my new clothes. No questions ever asked either by the security at the entrance or at the Front Desk.

In the morning, if going to work with Dr. Kennedy, I would dress like a foreigner, with clothes I now collected in my wardrobe. Most of the time I would return in a taxi. No matter how late I returned home, I would see my mother sitting in the sofa in the living room and waiting for me.

"Shao-nian," one morning seeing me leaving in western clothes, "Could you stop doing this?" my mother asked me in a more concerned manner than demand. "Every morning when you walking away, my heart is gone with you too. Every evening, I wait for you by the window sill, fearing the most: that the police will arrest you today."

"Mom, I will be OK." I assured her and walked out fast. I stopped outside the door for a second, then I picked up a small chalk end in the tray of the black notice board hung in the landing of the stairway. It was used by the Neighborhood Committee to write revolutionary slogans With Cultural Revolution winding down, the board was most time blank, no more Mao's quotation written on it.

I paused for a second, then wrote down on the board: *bugan guran bunong shibai* (of course doing nothing can avoid failure), *maoxian cainong chenggong* (Taking risk is the only way to succeed). I put down the calk end and walked off.

Before Dr. Kennedy left China, he took me to the Bank of China's head office which was situated just beside *Tiananmen Square*. He opened a bank account under *US-*

China Education Foundation, and had my signature authorized, so that I was the person to draw money for the activities in Beijing! I became their official representative in Beijing. Dr. Kennedy told me that I could use taxi anytime I work for him, Dr. Kennedy understood that was a necessary protection: it would be odd for me wearing western clothes and fighting to get on a bus, a sure way to get attention of a police. I could eat at the restaurant of my choice, though *US-China Education Foundation* never gave me a salary, I had a free-hand to draw money and use. I must have gained enough trust from Dr. Kennedy by my working with him in short period.

I was instructed to visit Beijing University and Beijing Ethic College to inspect the students dormitory and to prepare for the coming American students for the program arranged with those schools.

Only two days after I saw Dr. Kennedy and Denise off at the airport, I got a telex from Albert, he would be arriving in Beijing the following day! He would be staying at Friendship Hotel again this time

I went to the airport with taxi to meet him that day after work. At that time, there were only a handful passengers arriving from each International flight. I quickly spotted Albert limping out of the exit gate, he gave me a hug and a kiss on my cheek, then went onto explained that he slipped on stairs and hurt his ankle at Seoul airport.

When we arrived at the hotel it was getting late. Going with Albert to Friendship Hotel was no longer a dread for me, I became confident and comfort with my appearance as Maria Woo, I did not worry that the security at the gate would stop me from entering the hotel.

Albert got his room assigned at the reception desk, it was in a different building, luckily the building was not far, just a short distance of walk from the main building, Albert did not even need a porter to take his language to the room, his only had one briefcase and small suitcase. we walked along the road to the other building. Friendship hotel was a big walled compound, with several buildings connected by road with flowers, bushes, trees, it was also a residence place for foreign experts and their families.

We entered the building, it was more like an apartment building, quiet, no lobby, just stairs and an elevator. We got to the second floor, found the room, Albert opened the door, I followed in behind him, he set down his small black leather suitcase, a little bigger than the one he bought for me during last trip, he then put down his briefcase in a bed, there were two twin beds in the room.

When he turned around, he embraced me in his arms, "Maria, darling, I thought of you all the time, this is why I come back, just for you." Albert pressed his lips over mine, I froze in his arms, I could feel the softness of his lips, but I did not know how to respond. My previous experience with *Jin Zheng*, *Wang Junxiang*, and *Xiao Lin* did not involved in the art of kissing. I simply stood motionless in Albert's arms. My memory of Albert's kiss was softness, not intruding. I was never a kisser, I hate someone sticking a tongue into my mouth. For me, true romance or love can be the meeting of the eyes, or holding of hands, or cuddling together over a bowl of popcorn in sofa.

Albert did not give me time to think more, he walked me toward the bed, then he was on top of me, I did not resist him, I was wearing the purple woolen dress, that was convenient for Albert, he pulled up my dress, he loosened his belt and pulled down his trousers … his penetrating was gentle, no pain at all, and then it was over. Albert was fast at love making, same as his business dealings. He abhorred dithering manner in any dealings in life.

Afterward, Albert got himself more comfortable, he opened his suitcase, and pulled out a pair of jeans. "Here, Maria, I got this for you in soul." he threw it to my hands, later on I learned that Albert was not a man of words when it came to woo a woman, he shower them with gifts, which was easier for him, because he had the money to buy.

I was very happy to see a pair of jeans for me! No Chinese wearing jeans at that time, only foreigners wore jeans. Albert continued to pull out more stuff from his small black suitcase, he was like a magician, I was his audience: a black swimming suit with bright turquoise blue and emerald green flower print on it, a piece of Scottish woolen tartan, with dark green, grey pattern, another piece of tartan with red, black, white, yellow pattern. "You can have these made into dresses by tailors here." Albert advised me about Scottish tartans.

When we finally sat down in chairs and I talked about my involvement with *US-China Education Foundation*, and Dr. Kennedy, Albert was all for it. Albert started talking about his life in England, his second wife Annett has a boutique shop, but they were not lived together any more, Annett had a son from her previous marriage... "Maria, I want to marry you." Albert told me in a manner of a business decision. "It will take some time for my solicitor to finalize my divorce with Annett." "I want to see your family again, tomorrow?" he added.

I told Albert that my father was in town too, he said that he was looking forward to meet his future father-in-law, Albert never forgot his kidology.

The next day was Sunday, Albert and I first went shopping, at that time there were no jewelry shops after Cultural Revolution. We visited a couple of antique shops near Qianmen and xuanwumen area, that was the old inner city area, many antique shops located in that area. Albert finally bought an gold ring set with a blue sapphire in cabochon cut, the sapphire was over 3 carat, the ring cost 450 *yuan*, much more than my whole year's salary at *China Daily*.

When we stepped outside the shop, Albert handed the ring box to me:"Maria, this is for you." I was taken back by such an expensive gift, I shook my head, "I don't want it, it is too much. Give this to your mother." I commented.

"Don't be silly, Maria," Albert almost laughed by my comment, "My mother will not wear this. I bought this for you. I want to marry you."

We went to Beijing Hotel to rest and have tea, there Albert struck a talk with a man with British accent, he was the manager for Midland Bank's new office in Beijing. Lance was in his late 30s or 40s, middle height, normal built, not sporty, nor fat. But his hair certainly receded faster than his age. His boald was prominent at the first sight. Lance wore a pair of rimless glasses.

Albert introduce me to Lance and told him that an from Beijing. Lance scanned at me up and down, and starting talking to me in Chinese. His Chinese was even better than Robin and other foreign students I met. I replied in English. That was the rule set, when Lance talked to me, it was always in Chinese, I replied always in English. I wanted keep my identity as Maria Woo.

During their talk, Lance mentioned that *Maxima* a French restaurant just opened for business in town, it was not too far from Beijing hotel. That settled it, Albert invited Lance to have dinner with him, me and my father.

The evening came, we arrived at *Maxima*, Lance was there at the bar already. Maxima was the talk of the town among the expatriates in Beijing, it was so expensive, many times more than Jianguo hotel! Only a few foreign diplomats would go there at the expense of their states.

The interior decoration was rich, heavy, and dark, the French manager greeted us at the table with his team of waiters, all in stiff starched white jackets and black bow ties. We were the only customers at the table in the dinner room then, I thought maybe we were early, but as the night went on, I realized that we were the only customers for that night. I took a good look at the heavy bonded menu book, I wanted to see how expensive Maxima could be, but to my surprise, there was no price printed on the menu. "Well, I should not bother asking for the price then, as I am not the one paying the bill." I thought, "Still it is odd, that there is no price printed on the menu."

The whole waiting team showered us with their hospitality, wine glasses were never empty, by the late night, Albert could not stop call my father "Baba, Baba ... " Lance finally stopped talking in Chinese to impress my father. Lance was relaxed then, he told us that he studied Chinese in Taiwan for three years, that was the reason he landed Beijing Office position from Midland Bank. He even married a girl from Taiwan without the blessing of the girl's father. He said when things were all arranged, he would bring his Taiwan wife to Beijing too.

When we finally finished dinner, Albert paid the bill with his credit card, the bill must have been big enough that the French manager awarded us with free taxi service!

Monday I went back to work at China Daily, when I walked into the Reference Room, I saw the papers on my desk piled high, I knew the others probably were watching my reaction, I did not say any words, simply sat down, starting moving: reading, cutting, pasting, filing, by noon time, the pile on my desk was gone. It was my principle, no matter how many sick notes I might have handed in, I always completed my share of work, no burden to others.

Albert spent a week in Beijing, he invited my whole family again to Jianguo hotel, the whole gang, there were six or seven of us, plus Albert, this time at Four Seasons restaurant in Jianguo, it was opened lately, it served fine Chinese food, everyone ate his heart full, we literally cleaned all the plates on the table!

When Albert left Beijing, he asked me to speak to my father about the marriage to him. One evening seeing my father sitting in the sofa content after the dinner, I thought it was a good time to speak to him, "Baba, Albert mentioned of marrying me while he was in Beijing this time."

"Buxing (cannot be done)." my father uttered the simple words in a normal but firm tone, he did not even look at me. I knew my father, he was a man of few words, but when he spoke, they were set in stone.

Work at *China Daily* was normal, but outside *China Daily*, I was working for *US-China Education Foundation* in my spare time. One day, *Zhao Xiaoliang* walked into the office, "Wu Shaonian, the security office wants to see you in their office." he announced it. Everyone looked up from their desk with curiosity in their eyes. "Security office" it did not sound good.

I walked upstairs and knocked at the door of the Security Office, and walked in. The Security officer was behind his desk, he threw a copy of *People's Daily* down on the desk in front me. "*Wu Shaonian*, have you read this news?" he pointed at the paper and asked.

I took up the copy pretending reading it, it was yesterday's copy. Of course I had read it, it was part of my work, reading other newspapers to file. A big news on the front page was the story of a team of policemen forced into a room at *Jainguo* hotel, they caught a French diplomat with his Chinese girlfriend in the room red-handed. The girl was sentenced to prison, and the French diplomat was expelled.

"We all know that you have contact with foreigners." the security officer said, "You are different from the rest here. You sometimes wear jeans. Your ears are pierced. You sometimes have lipstick on." the officer started counting my offences.

Yes, I did have my ears pierced, so that I could wear earrings easily, that was for the role of Maria Woo. I did sometimes have faint lipstick on, that was all from my protection from police when I played the role of Maria Woo.

"Wu Shaonian," the security officer said, "The government put this news on the front page, this is called "*sha ji gei hou can"* (kill the chicken in front of a monkey), it is government's policy, no Chinese are allowed to have liaison with foreigners!"

"Sometimes you called sick leave, we knew that you were not sick, where did you go, who were you with in those days?"

"You need our permission before you can have contact with a foreigner!"

"From today on, I order you to report to me of any activities that you do with foreigners, you will hand to me for any correspondences you receive from foreigners!"

The security officer bombarded me with his orders, his palms started pounding on the desk. I stood there waiting for him to finish his orders, "Fine, if you can write down these orders in big letters and post them at the entrance of the building, I will hand you my foreign mail." I said defiantly and left his office.

The next day, there was no notice from the security officer posted on the entrance wall about me having to surrender my foreign mail. But the security officer started calling me upstairs to his office every the other day, demanding me to report my activities after work. His harassment went of for two or three weeks.

One day he ordered me to be in his office. He started his routine demand, "Wu Shao-nian, have you received any mail from foreigners? Did you meet any foreigners without our permission?"

I looked into his eyes, "Today I am resigning from China Daily!" I said.

His draw simply dropped, he did not know how to respond to my bombshell. I knew I was probably the first in the whole country to resign from a government position. It was simply unthinkable.

After a few seconds of silence, the security officer said: "Ok, I will talk to the authorities, we will inform you of our decision on your resignation."

The next afternoon almost at the end of the day, I was called up to the security officer' office. "Wu Shaonian, our authority accepted your resignation request. You are released from China Daily today." he announced the moment I entered his office.

This time I was speechless for a few seconds. "That's it?" that was all I could utter at his announcement.

"That is it." the security officer said with a triumphant smile on his face, they finally got

Rid of the only Christian working there.

"I can just leave, and go home? No paper to sign?" I asked to reconfirm his statement.

"Nope. That is it. You can leave today." the security officer said without any emotion on his face.

I turned around, stepped out of his office, and walked down stairs to the reference room. I started collected my personal stuff, and my little bed roll, the others in the office asked what happened. I told them that I resigned, they looked at me in disbelieve. I knew I must look like a biggest fool in the world in their eyes. Nobody resign from a government, let alone resigning from a coveted elite *China Daily*.

The bus ride home that evening seemed longer than usual, my hands were full, carrying bed roll, wash basin and other stuff. I opened the door, and stepped inside my mother's apartment. "Mom, I am back."

"Shaonian, why are you carrying all your stuff back?" my mother asked with big concern on her face.

"I resigned from *China Daily*, mom." I set bed roll down in the sofa and told her the news.

"What? What are you talking about?" my mother did not believe her ears.

"I resigned from China Daily! Mom." I looked up to her and repeated my announcement.

"Shaonian, you're crazy!" my mother cried out, "How could this happen? I thought you loved working at *China Daily*. You fought many years to study English, and finally you got a good job at *China Daily*. How could you throw all this away? How can you survive in the society without a job?"

"Mom, look at me," I assured her with my hands spread out, "I have two hands, I can make a living, I will survive!"

After saying this, the reality suddenly sunk in, I had not yet planned my survival, but somehow I had confidence. "From now I have no one to answer to! I am free like a bird in the sky, in a communist country!" The realization was exuberating but the same time frightening.

"Lord, You are my protector, You are my provider. Amen!" I prayed that night before I fell asleep.

Chapter 23

US-China Education Foundation

The first group of US students came to Beijing near the end of 1982, as the result of meetings with Beijing Ethnic College. I was US-China Education Foundation's representative in China to oversee that all the students welfare while they're studying in Beijing, It was Foundation's short term study group.

There were about 8 of them, coming from different states in US, I remembered Karen, a big size lady, and Barry a small man came from Alaska. There was a student Nasaji (I forgot his name by now) , coming from Japan! His father was a well-known politician in Japan at that time, how he managed to join US-China Education Foundation's first program in Beijing was a mystery to me, but I never asked Dr. Kennedy. They would study Chinese for two months in Beijing.

I could talk directly to the head of their Foreign Affairs Office, Mr. Xu, though I did not stay at the students dorm, I went to the college every day if the students had any requests, I would talk to Mr. Xu.

Among the group, there was Dr. Kennedy's daughter Jojan, medium height, with long dark hair flowing down her shoulder, she had the mix-racial children's trace, her mother was a Chinese! But her mother left her while she was a child, though there was Chinese connection in her blood, she never have any experience of Chinese culture, she was a typical American girl. Since Jojan was the daughter of Dr. Kennedy, she had the privilege of having her own room, the rest of the group all shared their rooms with a roommate.

Jojan was more a tomboy girl, she did not care much of wearing nice clothes, as a matter of fact, I was the one in the group, always wearing nicer clothes than the rest of the students, as for my role protection. Poor Mr. Xu, dealing with me during that time, never figured out that I was a local girl, living only 2 miles down the road!

Jojan was always in a baggy man's shirt, a pair of sweat pant, no make up. She did not like the food served at the cafeteria, I managed to get a small electrical burner in her room, we often cooked noodles in her room.

My memory of those two month program was quite vague now, there was not much after class activities. The college was very cautious at that time since it was their first time to have foreign students on their campus. One day Jojan talked about going to Great Wall, but not the tourist section. It was near *Miyun* Reservoir, a dilapidated section of Great Wall, I heard about it from local people, but never visited that area before.

Miyuan was an outer county of Beijing's municipality, to get there we had to travel by train. I did not talk to Mr. Xu about this activity, knowing that he would not approve it, because *Miyun* was a sensitive military zone, no way they would allow foreigners to visit there. When I looked at the map, it appeared that the section of the Great Wall was not too far from the train station, we could get off the train, and trek a couple of miles and climb the Wall.

The plan was set, we did not tell all other students except few, otherwise if it leaked out, the school might stop us. It would be only Jojan, Nasaji, the Japanese student, Josh and me: the gang of four! One weekend, we got up early, while the dorm was quiet, everyone on that floor was still asleep.

We tiptoed, whispered to gather at the meeting point downstairs, then single filed walked out of the school. With an early bus, we arrived at Beijing railway station. The 45 minutes train ride outside Beijing was uneventful, since it was early, the train was not crowded, we got off *Miyun* station. I looked at the map again, the section of Great Wall should not be too far from the *Miyun* station, we could simply walk there along a road for a couple of miles, then get off the road, to climb the mountain.

We walked out of the small station, set off for the hike on the winding road leading to the mountains. The gentle breeze with early morning sun instilled us with high spirit, our steps filled with bounces, we felt like young kids, we talked loud, laughed loud, with our arms spreading out. The road was empty, occasionally a farm truck would pass by, the driver and others on the truck would turn their heads toward us, an unusual sight at that time: Josh was a tall and slim, pale skinned Caucasian with blond wavy hair, Jojan a tall brunette with striking beautiful face. Nasaji could pass as a Chinese, and me a small Chinese girl.

But our jubilation was short lived, 30 minutes after our bouncing and laughing on the road a jeep came up behind us. When it stopped by us, two police men stepped off the jeep! They asked us what we were doing in *Miyun*, if we had permission from *Gonganju* (the public security bureau).

Within minutes, we, the *gang of four* were cramped into the police jeep and heading backward!

We passed the train station, the police jeep kept going, then soon it stopped at the police station, which was not far from the train station. Once inside the station, a senior police man in duty told us that as soon as we got off the train, someone at the station had reported us to the police station. *Miyun* was a highly sensitive military zoon, we were the first foreigners stepping off the train at *Miyun* station!

I was the only one who spoke Chinese, I told the senior police man that we were students from US-China Education Foundation studying at Central Ethical College, I had a paper with the college and Foundation's stamps on. We were very lucky, the senior policeman looked at my paper, and decided to let us go. He told us he would contact with the college of our unauthorized trip the following week.

"The next train going back to Beijing will arrive in 2 hours, you should take your students back on that train." the senior policeman ordered me. "Haode (OK)." I answered with my head nodding down several times.

We walked out of the police station, heading back to the railway station. Since the next train would arrive in 2 hours, the railway station was deserted, no one around, while waiting, we decided to try our luck. We all waited outside the station at the spot not be seen by people.

We saw buses passing through the road, when a bus heading toward the mountain came, we waved it down, dashed toward the bus, within seconds, we were on the road toward the mountain! "Please, please, God, let no policeman seeing us!" I secretly prayed that police jeep would not trail the bus.

After 20 minutes bus ride, the bus conductor let us off the bus, he said if we wanted to climb the Great Wall that was the spot to start. The mountain rose right up by the roadside. We could see the section of the Wall on top of the mountain. We did not waste time, "Come on, let us disappear in the mountain before others could see us." I urged others.

We started the climb, the terrain was rugged, rocky, but for us young and strong, no peak was unattainable! Gradually the space between us four spread out, Jojan was the head of the group, *Nasaji* was trailing right behind her, Josh was not as strong as Jojan, he started puffing, panting, I decided to stay with Josh and be the tail of the group. If police came after us, I would be the one to face them, I reasoned myself.

I shouted to Jojan: "Jojan, go ahead, we will meet you on the Wall." Soon I could not see Jojan and *Nasaj*i any more, the terrain, the rock, the winding path swallowed them.

Now just me and tall Josh. Josh was not in a hurry, he started telling jokes to me, American jokes, I was slow at jokes and punchlines, till this day, I could not laugh with those stand up comedians. But Josh's jokes made the climb easy.

When we finally made up to the first section of the Great Wall, *Jojan* and *Nasaji* were waiting for us there. This section of the Great Wall was not open to the public, it was in a original state, loosen bricks, fallen walls, it required cautious to walk along this section, it stretched out to mountains as far as our eyes could see! It was already passed the noon time, the detour to the police station took time off our planned climbing schedule.

Our food supply was meager, I had boiled tea eggs prepared the night before at home, two tea eggs for each person. Jojan brought along with her a few popular American chocolate bars, one for each. We all had a bottle of water with us. We sat down, ate the eggs, chocolate bar.

It must be around 2 or 3 o'clock, Jojan said the she would like to explore a little bit more further down the Great Wall seemed stretching endlessly, Nasaji said he would go with Jojan. Josh was content resting there, and watching the mountains. I hesitated for a second, then I consented, "Jojan, please keep time in mind and be careful." I reminded Jojan before she and *Nasaji* walked away.

Just Josh and me and the Great Wall. We sat and watched layers of mountain ranges, no more American jokes from Josh, no more laughs from Jojan.. just the mountains, the "Wall" and us. Though it was silent at that moment, I could feel the powerful energy at that spot seemed billowing to me internally. We were definitely recharged after sitting on top of the Wall, time seemed warped into eternity.

When I checked my watch it was about 4 o'clock in the afternoon, I turned toward Josh: "Josh, I think that we should head back down the mountain, we still have to catch a train and travel back to Beijing."

"What about Jojan and *Nasaji*?" Josh asked, "I hope they can come back soon." I looked toward the direction they left and commented.

 stood up, held up my palms to my mouth to form a loudspeaker, "Jojan nnn.... Nasaji iii....." I called their names out to the mountains with all my lungs capacity, the mountains echoed back, surely they could hear my calling.

"Josh, I think we should start heading down the mountain now, otherwise, it will be too dark for us to get back to the road." I said to Josh, "I hope *Jojan* and *Nasaji* hear my calling and heading back too."

There is a saying; "*Shangshan rongyi, xiashan nan* (going up hill is easy, going down hill is hard." It was an absolute truth. It took Josh and me more than 1 hour to get down to the road, during our descend I kept looking back hoping to spot Jojan and *Nasaji*, when we finally put our feet down on the level ground next to the road, there was still no sight of Jojan, and *Nasaji*, it was getting dark fast, Josh and I sat on a big rock by the roadside waiting for them, finally they appeared just before the last fable light in the sky fading away. I sighed with a big relief, "Come on, let's get going back to the railway station!" I urged them, "I hope we catch a train back to Beijing."

The darkness descended, in that remote area, there was not street light, we walked along the dark road, moon did not come up yet, luckily the was some faint light in the sky, we walked toward the railway station which was small cluster of specks of light twinkling in the distance.

No vehicles, or buses passing by us, our spirit was subdued, we dragged our feet in the darkness, no one was talking, when we finally walked into the railway station, to our dismay, the last train to Beijing had left 30 minutes ago. I did not want us to linger at the railway station too long, someone might report us to the police station again, then we could be in a big trouble, because early in the day the senior policeman told us to go back to Beijing right away.

We decided to hitch hike back to Beijing. Four of us, walked back into the darkness of the road, soon we saw lights beamed from behind, we turned back, waved our hands, jumped up and down, the vehicle passed us, and then slowed down, and stopped by the roadside, we all cheered out loud and run toward it.

It was a farm truck with a long loading bed, the sides of the bed was built up with wooden planks about one and half meter high, like those used to transport cattle. The truck bed was filled with turnips right up to the edge. It was heading to *Beijing*'s wholesale market.

The driver said there was no seats for us in his cabin, we would have to climb up to stay on top of truck bed. "That is not a problem at all. Uncle, as long as you can take us back to Beijing, we have classes tomorrow morning." I said eagerly to the driver.

We climbed up to the top of the truck's bed, and settled down with turnips. The truck started moving, we could finally stretch out our legs and leaned back with turnips to relax. The cool evening air rushed by, it felt good. Only by then I felt the hungry pain in my stomach, I picked up a turnip, wiped it clean on my pants, and took a bite on it. Hmm.. It tasted sweet, crisp! Everyone followed my suit...

After more than two hours, the truck entered Beijing, we got off the farm truck at a convenient bus stop, by the time we finally walked into the dorm building at the campus, everyone was already asleep. "Thank God," I thought to myself, "Otherwise how do you answer questions if any one sees us in soiled clothes by laying with turnips atop of a farm truck."

I was really relieved a few days later when no words from the Foreign Affair Office inquiring about our trip to *Miyun*. Obviously the senior policeman at *Miyun* station did not follow up as he said. God was good to us. After *Miyun* trip, *Jojan* and *Nasaj*i became inseparable, eventually, Sasaji went to US to study in the school where Jojan was in, and they finally got married.

Meantime, Albert continued his pursuit on me, though he was thousands of miles away in England. I started receiving letters from him, when I got mail from him, it would be a stack of letters: he was writing to me every day! Later on when I met Olga, his secretary in Albert's office, she told me that Albert never wrote letters by hand, he always dictate his letters, she was pleased to meet me, the Chinese lady who stole his heart.

I responded to Albert's love letters, though I was not in love. I am the person that if you treat me well, I will return it two times, three times more. Albert was a man with means, not only he wrote to me everyday, he started sending me gifts: I received custom hand made high heel shoes from England, a floral dress from *Harrods* in London, a gold *Longines* watch ...

The day when I put on the dress from *Harrods*, supported with a pair of white shoes with inch and half high heels (first time to wear high heel shoes), my tipsy walk across the students cafeteria floor drew the attention from all the American students.

Josh blew a long whistle, I started giggling while trying to maintain my balance with head up at the meantime, suddenly Paul, Josh's roommate got up from his table, he dashed toward me. Paul was as tall as Josh, 6 feet 2, also with moping curly hair, but his hair was dark brown, he was a physically strong young man, he looked like Tom Selleck in the movie, but younger.

Paul grabbed my arms and twisted them behind me, "Hey," Paul called to the rest of the students, "Let's kidnap Maria, let's demand big ransom from fat Englishman Albert!" by then the whole crowd let out a roaring laughter ....

My work with US-China Foundation proceeded with no problem, I learned my lesson, no more trips outside Beijing. The two months seemed came to the end fast, the day when I went with students to the airport to see them off, I made a wish: one day I will be the one leaving and getting on a plane, not just seeing others off. May God hear my wish.

Chapter 24

Bye, China

The US-China Education Foundation was the forerunner after the lifting of Iron Curtain in China, it not only organized first groups of American students to study in China, Dr. Kennedy also arranged Christian organizations to come to China under the Foundation's program.

In early spring 1983, Dr. Kennedy came to Beijing, when I went to the Beijing Capital Airport to meet him, I saw Dr. Kennedy walked out with two other Americans. From his brief introduction, I learned that Jim was the president of *Youth For Christ International*, and Bob, Jim's friend, was a philanthropist, Both Jim and Bob were in their late 50's, both were over 6 feet tall, both had full grey hair, both were physically fit, not thin or heavy, but fit, beside their different facial features, they were like brothers, when I visited them the next morning at the hotel, they both came in with their tracksuits after their morning jogging. That was a big difference with Dr. Kennedy, I never saw Doc. doing anything physical, always meetings, talks, or eating, that was why he was heavy.

Jim and Bob stayed in Beijing only for four days, I went with them to Great Wall, Forbidden City, their trip resulted in an agreement which *Youth for Christ International* would send their young students to US-China Education Foundation's program in China at various universities. But there were some strict rules for their Christian students, no aggressive evangelism. It had to be done by cultural exchange form, sharing experience. No preaching of any kind on the campus. No bible distribution, no any Christian literature distribution, only by personal experience sharing.

In summer 1983, together with *Youth for Christ International*, the US-China Foundation, brought an athletic youth group called *All Star* basketball team from US. Their arrival at the airport was a scene, they were tall by any standards, but to Chinese eyes, they were giants. Though they were all from *Youth for Christ*, we did not made it known to Chinese authority, the *All Star* players were only as friendship exchange program for young American athletes.

The basketball team stayed at *Yanjing* hotel, their stay was a short one-week program, they would play with Chinese young basketball teams. One morning, after breakfast in the dinning hall of the hotel, Dr. Kennedy asked me to do a presentation of young Christians in China, I talked about my own experience of becoming a Christian, our bible study, our church... at the end of my talk I was applauded by thunderous clapping of those giants. I still have photos of that morning, with me standing with giant players, and their coach, the coach was only to their shoulder height, and my standing tall barely above their waist height.

Youth for Christ International continued their youth in our program, we embedded their students with regular students from US, only me knowing who was from *Youth for Christ International*, I monitored their evangelist activities, no public preaching, Christianity could only be shared through personal contact with Chinese students. For the security and safety of US-China Education Foundation, I didn't even go with them to our church, I did not bring them to my bible study group. These a few Youth for Christ students would have to have their own experience of life in China. I think that was the wise decision I made, even though I was a fearless zealot for Christ at that time.

Around late summer 1983, Pastor Can announced in our church that Nanjing Christian Seminary was allowed to reopen in that autumn, Beijing churches were to select two young Christians to go to Nanjing Seminary, obviously after that they would become pastors working in Beijing. Anyone in our church could apply for this, we were all excited for this news, my bible study group members urged me to apply, of course I would love to go to Nanjing, I would love to devote my life to Christianity. I applied to the church and all young people at the church were anxious to see who would be selected by pastors to go to Nanjing.

We did not have to wait for long, since the Seminary would be open in September. When Pastor Can announced two names who were selected by the church to go to Nanjing, I was not one of them. I felt disappointed and discouraged, my involvement with church was decreased after that, though I continued with bible study group, I no longer visited church every Sunday as I did.

When I told Dr. Kennedy about my disappointment of not being selected for Nanjing Seminary, he mentioned maybe he could arrange a seminary for me in US. Dr. Kennedy talked with Jim and Bob of Youth for Christ International, both of them volunteered to be my sponsors to finance me for a seminary in US. A month later, I received a big package from US of my enrollment to a seminary in US, all I needed to do was to go to American embassy to apply for a student visa.

I was overjoyed for a few minutes, then the reality hit me. In order to go to American embassy, I needed a passport, which I did not have. In early 80s for an ordinary Chinese person to apply and get a passport was like "waiting for stuffed pancakes falling from the sky", almost impossible!

I remembered a few years back, when my family ridiculed me by the dinner table for my obsession of English study, when I told them that one day I would have a little red book called passport in my hands, they all burst into laughs with rice spilled out of their mouths ...

Since I had no government work unit to apply for a passport, I had to go to local police station to apply for a passport, I showed them my American school's paper, I needed a passport to go to American Embassy to get a visa, they said that I needed to go to municipality's security bureau, which was in downtown Beijing, actually not too far from Beijing Hotel at that time. It reminded me that many times, I fooled those security people at Beijing hotel, by wearing Western clothes, speaking English only.

I went to Municipality Public Security Bureau, I presented all my papers, filled endless forms with personal information from when I was in kindergarten, family background dated back to my grandfather *Clay Pot Wu*, they told me to go back a month later to find out their decision. After a long month's of waiting, I went to Public Security Bureau, when my turn came, they handed me all the papers back, and told me, that they would not issue me a passport, no reasons given, that was it. I stood there for a minute, then walked away. I knew it was no use arguing with them there, if their decision was no, that was it. I had to find other way around.

I talked to different people looking for *guanxi* (connection) with Public Security Bureau Foreign Affair Department, I hoped to find a way to get a passport. Finally through friends' friends, I actually did not know this lady at all, but words passed out, the date was set for me to meet her to get information concerning my passport application.

I remembered that day, I met her at a bus stop not too far from Municipal Public Security Bureau. Once we introduced each other, I could feel the information was not going to be positive, she did not have any smile on her face.

"Wu Shao-nian," she started talking, "Your case is a difficult one. Do you know you were on Bureau's watch list as dangerous to young people, and having unauthorized connections with foreigners. They will never let you leave the country."

I looked into her eyes, she was not joking, she was simply deliver the information she got from her friend in the Bureau. My heart was sunk, there was no need to ask her for more details, I thanked her for the trouble of getting the information for me and we parted at the bus stop. I waited for another bus to go home, when the bus came, I looked around and stepped onto the bus, wondering if I was followed by the Bureau people then

Once on the crowded bus, I held tight to the hand rail, my mind was racing: "Maybe after all the Public Security Bureau was not that dumb as I imagined, maybe they had been following me all the time, maybe *Miyuan* police did report to the school or to the Bureau, maybe the church reported my bible study group to the Bureau, maybe my bible distribution was noted by the Bureau, maybe… maybe…"

I was crushed by the lady's report of me being on the Bureau's black list. "Should I quit what I have been doing?" I asked, but I knew myself, I would not quit. At the meantime, I knew that I had no chance to get a passport through Beijing Municipal Public Security Bureau.

To get a passport it had to be a miracle from God, "God, protect me from any danger, God, please help me with a passport." I prayed silently as usual, I normally did not repeat my request from God, once said, I knew it was delivered, my part was having faith, having patience and waiting for God's timing not mine.

I gave up on studying in a seminary either in Nanjing or America, apparently God did not want me to be a pastor in a church, I reasoned. As long as God protected me, the Public Security Bureau could not put me in prison, then I would continue living my life as it had been.

Beside working for US-China Education Foundation, I got another part time job with a Japanese trading Company. I met Chieko Fujita at Beijing Hotel. That day I was waiting in line for some service there, Chieko was behind me, we were just chatting casually, then Chiako asked me if I was from Hongkong, what company I was working for. I could not help of giggling seeing Chieko's facial expression of shock, when I explained to her of US-China Education Foundation, and I was from Beijing, I was a local girl! By the end Chieko asked if I could visit her company's office in *Xinqiao* hotel the following day. I accepted the invitation.

Next day I went to *Xinqiao* hotel, which was not too far from Beijing hotel, it was a smaller hotel, If *Jianguo* hotel was the five-star hotel for top business men then, Beijing hotel was for foreign journalists, and foreign residents, then *Xinqiao* was for people from *Hongkong*. But it was still a nice hotel. My memory of hotels at that time was they had bathrooms with real bath tubs.

When I was a small girl, whenever my father stayed at hotels, Beijing or Xinqiao, because of Government's conference there, we children would go to visit him, and spent long time in the hot bath tub in his room. Because back at our own apartment at that time, there was no bathtub in the bathroom, we all had to go to a public bath house to take showers once a week or once every two weeks.

It did not cost much to take a bath at a public bath house, 15 cents or less. You could spend 30 cents for a private tub with a small private bed attached to the tub. Mostly the private tubs were at men's section. When my father went out for a bath, I knew he was to take a real bath: private tub, then napping in a private bed, plus a pot of tea and massage. But for us girls, it was a big public shower room, with bare shower heads sticking out from four walls, no privacy of any thing, no curtain, no partial division board, just a big open room, every one, old, young or children, all naked standing around, shoveling to each other to get under a shower head....

At that time, my standard of luxury was judged by a private bath tub availability. Till this day, I am a bath person, by the end of the day, I have to have a hot bath, if for any reason, I could not have a hot bath, I would feel deprived.

From my father's conferences, I was quite familiar with *Xinqiao* hotel. Chieko's office was in a small room with two twin beds. There were a lot of papers, catalogues piles up on a desk. At that time, there was not a lot of trading between China and Japan yet, Chiako worked for her father's trading company after she graduated from a university in Michigan, she even showed me her American boy friend's photo while she was in US. Now she was in Beijing, her father's company's goal at the time was not to sell, but to gather information of trading with China, passing catalogues, to prepare the company for the opening of Chinese market.

We did not have a lot of paperwork to do, or meetings to attend. I ended more like a companion for Chiako wherever she went. Chiako was frugal, at least when I was working for her. No expensive meals at Jianguo hotel, not even at Beijing hotel. I could simply treat myself a meal at Beijing hotel if I wanted. But with Chiako, I played down scale, sometimes we simply had lunch at her office/room, she would cook Ramen noodles for us in the room. That was the first time I ate instant noodles. I was quite impressed by Japanese efficiency. When she opened her closet, beside piles up catalogues, there were piles up Ramen noodles! She could have been a Ramen noodle peddler in China then.

Sometimes we went out to have lunch on the street, it was noodles again. I was not a noodle person. My concept of Japanese people's food, through working with Chiako, was noodles, noodles and noodles. Chiako knew a small noodle restaurant not too far from Xinqiao hotel, when we got tired of eating Ramen noodles in her room, she would take me to that little hole on the wall noodle shop. She would order *Dandan mian* for us, one bowl of *Dandan mian* at that time was only 12 cents!

Dandan Mian was so spicy hot, I never learned to handle too spicy food, we two would sit on worn out wooden stools, our heads bent over a bowl of *Dandan mian*, though the noodles was always served cold, my face turned red, my tongue was on fire, I gasped for air to cool off my mouth, but it was a hot summer day, the hot air did not help much, the sweat drops started rolling down my face, Chiako could not stop giggling seeing me burned up. When we finally finished *Dandan mian*, I was soaked in my sweat, but strange enough, I actually felt cooled, the summer heat accumulated inside me was all evaporated out of me. From Chieko's *Dandan mian*, I learned a survival secret, if you were hot, wanted to cool off, drink a cup of hot tea, or a bowl of *Dandan mian* if available, sweat it out, you would be totally cooled off from within.

One day Chieko and I went to *International Club* to play tennis, it was near *Jianguo* hotel, more than twenty years passed, I passed it again while I was in Beijing, it was still there, only its look no longer appeared upper class as it once did. Chieko had a couple of her Japanese men friends there to play tennis with, of course they asked me to join them, I did a few strokes, but no luck, I could not control the ball, so I told Chieko that I would rather watch them playing.

After tennis, we all cramped into a taxi to go to Beijing hotel to have some ice cream. *International Club* was only ten minutes drive from Beijing hotel at that time, inside the taxi, her two Japanese male friends took out two small vials from their gym bags, they drank them, and joked that with ginseng and royal jelly power in those vials, they now had more energy. Later at Beijing hotel, I noticed that those ginseng royal jelly drink were available at the gift shop there, but they were priced so that no ordinary Chinese could buy them.

I never dreamed then that some twenty years later, when I owned a health food store, I would order a case of ginseng royal jelly drink, exact the same brand as in the gift shop at Beijing hotel, I could drink as many vials as I wanted. At the back room of my store, there were not only ginseng, but deer antler, cordycep, ganoderma, sea horse, gecko, even snake, soaked in vodka in big jars. In my past life, I must have been a medieval alchemist, cooking up different concoctions in the back room.

One morning in spring 1984, I read the headline on the front page of *People's Daily*: Chinese government issued a new law allowing Chinese citizens to marry to foreigners! I couldn't believe my eyes, I looked at those lines again, it was not mistake, the front page news by *People's Daily*, the No. I government propaganda paper! I sent telex about this news to Albert in England. The next day, I got a notice from postman, there was a telex for me to collect at the Central Telecommunication Building in downtown. I jumped onto my bicycle, and raced to the Telecommunication Building, I hurried into the hall with 20 feet high ceiling, the place was quiet, only a handful of customers there, I walked to the International Telex counter and handed the lady clerk the notice to collect the incoming telex for me. She handed me back an envelope, I opened the envelope, there on the page was the message from Albert: *I am coming to China to marry you.*

I stood there in the middle of the huge hall staring at the telex in my hands, my mind was raging with brain storm amid the stillness of the huge hall. "Though this is government's new law, since I was refused a passport application, since I was on Public Security Bureau blacklist, can I trust the municipality and their public Security Bureau to allow me to marry Albert?"

"What about moving out of Beijing? what about moving to my father's city *Taiyuan*? I don't think my name is listed there, plus with my father's high ranking position in that city, I probably will have more chances to get married and get a passport in Taiyuan..."

By the time I rode my bicycle back to my mother's apartment, my brain storm was over, my mind was clear.

I walked into the living room, and announced my decision to my mother: "Mama, I want to move my *hukou* (residence registration) to Taiyuan?" My mother looked up to my eyes to see if I was joking, but she knew at the same time in her heart that I was not joking, she knew her crazy head-strong daughter. I never talked jokes, what I said, they were already set in stones, no one would change my mind once the words got spoken by me.

"Why, Shao-nian?" my mother asked not to change my mind, but to know the reason behind this insane announcement. No body, at that era, nobody wanted to move Beijing *hukou* out, there was only one way flow, to get into Beijing. Thousands of married couples had to live thousands miles apart across China because one partner did not have *hukou* in Beijing. I had to bribe, produce fake medical documents to return to my home city.

"Mama, I just got telex from Albert, he wants to marry me! Though the government just changed the law to allow a foreigner to marry a Chinese, I did not want any problem for us from Beijing Public Security Bureau. If I move to a provincial city, we will have a better to succeed." I explained my reasons behind this suicidal move.

My mother hesitated for a minute, "You are taking a big risk, Shaonian, if it does not work, you won't be allowed to live in Beijing again!" she said and added: "You need to discuss this with your father." I did, I actually took an overnight train and arrived the next day at Taiyuan.

My father was always happy to see me, after all I was his favorite girl. I showed my father the clipping of the front page news from *People's Daily*, and the telex I received from Albert. "Baba, please, time has changed. Look, even the government changed the law. I want to marry to Albert, you met him, you liked him ..." I pleaded with my father for his blessings.

My father put his glasses down on the news clipping on the side table beside the sofa, he got up and headed to the kitchen, I followed him, waited without more words... without looking at me, he said: "If this is really what you want, if the government allows you, I will not stop you..." he paused for a couple of second, "Tell Albert, I will have him as my son-in-law." he said.

"Really? Baba!" I succeed the first step of getting his blessing for our marriage, then I pressed on, "Baba, can we get married in Taiyuan? The Central governmental law applies to all provinces, if I move my *hukou* to Taiyuan, surely we can get married in Taiyuan."

"Let me talk to my friends at Provincial Committee's office first! Moving your *hukou* to Taiyuan is a big decision." my father said.

"Please, Baba, ask them! Take the news clipping to them!" I urged him.

The next day, my father walked into my room and said to me, "Yes, they received the new law in their office too. They said, if you move to Taiyuan, you will be the first person in the province to marry to a foreigner, they would like to see this new law enacted. They will help you at all the levels."

"Baba, that is great, then I will go back to Beijing tomorrow, and start application of moving my *hukou* to Taiyuan."

The following weeks went like whirlwind, I said good-by to Chieko, I wrote to Dr. Kennedy of my upcoming marriage to Albert and my move to Taiyuan, they were happy for me, though they were sad that they would lose a great help of a local girl in Beijing.

Early summer, I moved to Taiyuan, my life in the provincial city was quiet, I spent most of my time in my father's apartment, reading, studying bible, doing chores for my father, I even stopped my wushu training, I wanted a low profile life, no adventures, no cause for attention from public security bureau in Taiyuan.

Every day, my father's apartment was drifted with Bible reading from a cassette player, in English of course. When I did laundry (there was no washing machine in household yet), I would put a cassette player on a little stool beside the big wash basin, while my hands pushing hard with a bed sheet on the rolling board, my ears were tuned to the Bible verses played on the little cassette player, earlier Dr. Kennedy brought me a Bible in a set of cassettes. I would also play a cassette from Albert, they were songs from Nat King Cole, among those songs was Albert's favorite one *Natural Boy*. Years later, though I heard many different rendition of *Natural Boy*, Nat King Cole is still the best for me.

Certain music or songs always remind me of my life in different time: my labor camp life, somehow was strangely connected with Romanian violin piece. With Albert, it is *Natural Boy*, with American students in college dorm in Beijing, it was the piano piece *Don't Cry for me, Argentina* by Richard Clayderman, which Jojan often played in her room, Schubert's *Ave Maria* always reminded me of my room in my mother's apartment, I connected the music with my English name Maria.

On day in late May, I got telex from Albert that he would be arriving in Beijing the coming week to marry me, I took a train back to Beijing the following week, and met him at the airport, I suggested that this time he should stay at Lido hotel, a new hotel chain by Holiday Inn, which was closer to Capital airport in Beijing. Lido hotel's lobby was very impressive, 20 feet chandelier cascading from high ceiling, the hotel was quiet compare to Jianguo hotel because it was just completed. I explained to Albert that we would get married in Taiyuan, instead of Beijing, Albert did not mind, so we took the next day train to Taiyuan.

There was only one hotel in Taiyuan which was allowed to accommodate foreigners, it was beside the city square, at that time very few foreigners had ventured into Shanxi province yet, of course *Taiyuan*'s hotel could not compete with those up in Beijing by foreign hotel chains. It was built in 60's for Russian experts working there. My father had already arranged us to meet relevant provincial official the next day.

The meeting with Mr. Zhang was quick, then we went there, Mr. Zhang explained the detailed procedure to have us registered. Albert needed to presented his divorce document validated by Chinese embassy in London. I had my divorce paper from Beijing, which was OK. Albert told Mr. Zhang that we would go back to Beijing, that when we had all the documents ready, we would meet Mr. Zhang again for final marriage registration.

We took a train back to Beijing. I preferred Lido hotel to other hotels, because people working at Lido hotel did not know my face. I did not want any attention from Beijing Public Security Bureau before my marriage to Albert. He took a room with twin beds, I spent day time with Albert at the hotel, but every night, I would return to my mother's apartment. We spent a lot of time in the hotel, reading in the room or walking outside the hotel in close proximity.

At that time, Lido hotel area was considered rural area outside downtown, there were only farmers' houses outside the hotel. Albert loved to play with goats at farmer's yards, and had photos with farmer's children, I still had photos of Albert playing with goats and kids, in farm fields.

Albert invited my family to eat at Lido hotel a few times, we did not go into the city, no more eating at fancy *Maxima* restaurant, or *Jianguo* hotel, we simply kept a low profile. Albert invited Lance from Midland Bank to Lido hotel to play chess in his room to kill time. It was a sight of these two English men, both partially bald heads, kneeling around a small bed, one with palm holding his chin, the other arms crossed around body, eyes glued to the chess board, I snapped that moment with a camera, the title should be: waiting time in Beijing.

Albert arranged DHL service to send his divorce paper back to his office in England, there his office manager Joe would personally take the document to Chinese embassy in London, to have it validated with Chinese embassy's stamp. After that Joe should send the validated document back to Beijing, then we should take the document back to Taiyuan.

A week passed, each morning when I walked into Lido hotel, went up to Albert's room, he would say: "Good morning, Maria, let's go down to the lobby to have breakfast." I knew then the document was not back yet by DHL.

On the 10th day morning, I walked into the lobby of Lido hotel, there, Albert was already waiting for me, with his hands behind him. "Good morning, Maria," he greeted me routinely, then he pulled out an oversized envelope hidden behind him, "DHL package is here." he added. We walked into the coffee shop in the lobby, we sat down, ordered breakfast, Albert opened the envelope, there it was the validated document with a Chinese Embassy's stamp!

I was overwhelmed by the reality: "I am getting married to Albert, I am leaving China!"

Flood of emotions, memories rushed out ... days in the Inner Mongolia, watching foreign movies in the frigid cold desert, with tears running down my face, yawning to go to the other side of the world... when I vowed in *Jin Zheng's* room in that small courtyard that I would go to far away land that *Jin Zhen* would never touch me again ... when I wished that I could be the one on the plane while I was at the airport seeing American students off... now it is happening for real, I am leaving China!

Suddenly I felt sick, when the waitress brought breakfast to our table, I could not eat any food, "Albert, could you finish breakfast alone, I need to go up to the room for a while." I said to Albert and put down the napkin. I hurried up to the room, and dashed to the bathroom, I wanted to vomit, though there was no food in my stomach... now I understand that how extreme emotional outburst can manifest in physical body.

A short while later, Albert came into the room, seeing my pale face, he asked:"Maria, what is wrong? Is this not what you wanted?" I smiled back to him and said: "Of course, Albert, this is what I have been waiting for a long time, I am just overwhelmed by the news, I will be fine after a while."

We did not waste time, we got on the earliest train to Taiyuan. My father was happy to see his soon to be son-in-law. Albert called him Baba like I did. Next day we went to Mr. Zhang's office, handed him the validated document along with my document, he examined them, and said he needed a few minutes, he left room with our documents, when he returned, he had a paper with him, it was marriage certificate with both of our names on it, he showed the paper to us to check the names, and he opened a drawer in his desk, took out a big round stamp, and he dabbed the stamp in a red ink pad, and pressed the stamp on the certificate.

There was no fireworks, no fanfares, no hands claps, only with presence of my father, my father's friend as witness, Albert, me and Mr. Zhang, but the history seemed paused for a moment, a moment of cheers! Mr. Zhang's stamp set the direction of the next milestone of my life journey, I knew at that moment that "I am heading West."

Once outside the provincial government's building, my father announced that he would cook a feast for our marriage the following evening. I decorated the dinner room at my father's apartment with colorful papers chains hung from the ceiling. That evening I wore a white blouse Albert bought for me, it had lace ruffles around collar and front, and skirt made with a red tartan material. There were around 20 people of my father's friends and neighbors. My father was happy that evening, so was Albert, even after all the guests left, they two continued their drinks of *erguotou*, a famed Chinese vodka, in my father's room without me, the interpreter, well, *erguotou* became their common language, they drank late into the night, when I went in to check on both men in my father's room, I snapped a shot of my father sitting in a sofa with his son-in-law Albert sitting next to him on the arm of the sofa, both smiled at my camera, with their wine glasses holding high, both with glassy eyes…

Albert spent three more days after our wedding at Taiyuan, then he left Taiyuan, this time I did not go with him to Beijing, he would stay at Jianguo hotel for one night before he flew out, he had several business meeting at other countries, all held off because of his waiting for the wedding in China.

As arranged with Albert, after our wedding which was around the end of June, I started applying for a passport right away at Taiyuan, as a wife of a British man, the provincial government had no intention to interfere with my quest for a passport, plus with my father's influence with his friends at upper level, I received my little red book within two weeks.

It was the beginning of July, 1984, I received my passport, a little red book. With my fingers running gently through the red cover of my passport, I remembered the evening when I announced by the dinner table with my family of my dream of having a little red book one day, and that comment caused uproar of laughter from my family ... yes, I am a believer of the power of a mind: if there is a will, there is way, as long as you have the patience, and the faith, walk the path, though it may bend or turn, many times.

There was no reason for me to stay in Taiyuan any more, I got married, I got my passport, I said goodbye to my father, I did not realize at that time, that as my life journey rolled forward with many more bends and turns, the next time, also the last time when I saw Baba in Beijing, it was in 1989, with my new American husband Bill Bates, it was during the students demonstration, and later on the Chinese army tanks rolled into *Tiananmen* square... the city was in turmoil during those days, we could feel the tension built up between the government and the students, my father urged Bill and me to leave Beijing before the army opened fire on students... we did, I said goodbye to my father, we left Beijing two days before army tanks rolled into *Tiananmen* square. That was the last time I said goodbye to my father.

With my little red book, I traveled back to Beijing, to apply visa to Sri Lanka, since Albert would having business meeting there at that time as he planned, I should meet him there, we could have our honeymoon in Sri Lanka, then flew to England.

While I was waiting for visa from Sri Lanka embassy, I kept a low profile life in Beijing, I spent most of my time in my room at my mother's apartment, reading, cleaning windows, washing bed sheets, no morning exercise, no church visit, no bible study activities, no visit with Beth Bauer, no visit to Chieko's office, no contact with US-China Education Foundation, no fanfare to people of my marriage to an Englishman, I did not even wear my fancy western clothes, I hoped that to Beijing Public Security Bureau, Wu Shao-nian simply disappeared, or vanished, they could relax a little bit then.

It took a week for me to collect my passport with visa stamped to visit Sri Lanka, it looked like that everything was in place as we planned, I sent telex to Albert: *Sri Lankan visa is obtained today.* His telex back: *we will send you airline ticket to Colombo by DHL.* Of course at that time, people traveled by paper tickets, there was no electronic ticketing yet.

On the fifth day after I got Sri Lanka visa, I received my airline ticket by DHL, it was the only International courier service allowed in China not too long ago. I studied the ticket, my plane date was on July 28th. I called my father in Taiyuan, and told him of the date of my leaving China, I asked him if he would come to Beijing to send me off, but he said it was not necessary, he said he would see me again.

I did not press him again, I knew my father, he was a reserved person, he did not like to show his emotions. To ask him to be at the airport seeing his favorite girl flying to a far away foreign land and not to show any emotions? That was asking too much from my father, he was not at my wedding to *Jin Zhen*, probably fearing of showing his emotions. But he was at my wedding with Albert, he cooked a feast, drank *erguotou* with Albert the whole night, that was enough as a father.

The departure day came, my mother and my sister, and brother went to the airport with me, I did not have much to take with me, just one small black leather suitcase Albert bought me, he said he would buy all the fancy clothes in

London when I arrived there. The taxi ride to airport seemed too soon, there was no crowd at that time, the huge check-in hall was very quiet. I found myself saying goodbye to my family, my mother had tears in her eyes, I did not cry, my heart and mind had already boarded the plane, I was ready to fly away, to be free like a bird in a bigger world.

I walked through the check-in counter, my family could not pass that, they waved me final goodbye. Then I picked up my hand carrying bag, proceeding to the boarding gate. I was there not very long when they announced the beginning of boarding of my plane, I approached the gate with my ticket, the airline staff at the boarding counter looked at my passport, the visa, the ticket, she paused for a few seconds, then she said to me: "Excuse me, Miss, could you please step on the side." she hinted me to step out of the line. Then she continued boarding other passengers, it was not a long line boarding the plane, it's destination was Hongkong, my first leg of journey to Colombo.

When the last passenger had boarded, I was still standing outside the line, though I did not say anything while waiting for all other passengers boarding, the internal dialogue was going fast: "now my family has already left the airport, they never guessed that I would be stopped at the boarding counter." "Is this Beijing Public Security Bureau final ambush to rein me in?"

Now she turned to me, she explained to me that there was a discrepancy of my travel plan. If I married to an Englishman, then I should fly to London, not Colombo. I explained to her of Albert having business meeting in Colombo, and us having honeymoon there, we would fly to London after our honeymoon. She told me to wait there, then she took my passport, my marriage certificate, ticket in hands and walked off!

It felt like eternity before she appeared with a man who she said was custom supervisor, this man explained to me that unless I signed a document prepared by Chinese custom at the airport, they would not let me board the plane. I said calmly: "OK, bring it on, show me the paper." inside me I was ready to sign on any paper, as long as I could board the plane.

The supervisor of the custom showed me the paper, it read like this: the Chinese government is not responsible for any mishaps happened to me if I fly to Colombo, Sri Lanka, because that is a third country, legally, it should not be on my travel plan...I am travelling at my own risk..." I picked up the pen he handed to me, and jotted down my name on the document in a flash of a second.

With signed paper in his hands, the custom supervisor handed me back my passport, marriage certificate, and waved to the airline lady who pulled me out, "She can board the plane now." he told her.

She handed me the ticket with boarding pass, then she said: "Hurry up, you are holding the plane from taking off!" I picked up my handbag, started walking toward the plane, I tried to be composed, I could see the stewardess standing at the door of the plane, waving to me to hurry up.

I started running, the scene was set in my memory forever: in slow motion I was running weightless almost like floating toward the plane ...

As soon as I boarded the plane, it took off. Sitting in my seat, I looked out of the window, the lush green fields, the clusters of farm houses, the city buildings, they became smaller and smaller, "Bye bye, China." I whispered in my heart.

Gradually the ground scenery was obscured by white clouds, I was above the clouds, it felt like I was in a dream, but I knew I was living this dream. It was a miracle that I was on this plane, "God, I believe in miracles, Amen!" I prayed.